A Gift For:

_____

From:

_____

WINTER COCKTAILS

Mulled Ciders, Hot Toddies, and Cocktail Party Snacks

{ BY MARÍA DEL MAR SACASA
PHOTOGRAPHS BY TARA STRIANO }

Hallmark

QUIRK BOOKS
PHILADELPHIA

This edition published in 2017 by Hallmark Gift Books, a division
of Hallmark Cards, Inc., Kansas City, MO 64141 under license from
Quirk Productions.
Visit us on the Web at Hallmark.com.

ISBN: 978-1-63059-843-3
1BOK1401

Made in China.
0717

Typeset in Ambroise, Sentinel, and Berthold Akzidenz-Grotesk

Designed by Katie Hatz with modifications by Hallmark
Prop styling by Penelope Bouklas and Emily Rickard

Photography by Tara Striano

Portrait on page 136 by Geraldine Pierson with makeup by
Lea Siegel at Ferny Chung Studios. Portrait on inside back
cover by Benoit Mouthon.

*Because of the risk of food-borne illness, raw or undercooked
eggs (and all food and drink recipes that contain them) should
not be served to little ones, older folks, expectant mothers, or
anyone who's immunocompromised. All other brave souls
ingest at their own risk.*

"Candy is dandy, but liquor is quicker."

—Ogden Nash, *Hard Lines*

Contents

Introduction

As the colder months approach, a dusky blue light insinuates itself ever earlier into the day and the wind's summer caress turns into a sharp reproach. Fall and winter may have their dreary stretches, but the glory of fiery-hued foliage and the hush of falling snow offer mesmerizing scenes and calming sounds. Gathering with friends at this time of year creates a comforting warmth that will hold us over 'til summer returns.

This book serves up the perfect antidote to any brisk day or frosty evening. It is broken down into categories, starting with seasonal classics like mulled ciders, wines, and hot toddies. These are followed by richer drinks, including spiky twists on eggnog and luxurious hot chocolates. Chilled drinks made warm with heady spirits and spicy ingredients also appear. A selection of recipes for small bites ensures the perfect party atmosphere.

The heart of this book may be the recipes, but its soul is the spirit of conviviality that is encouraged in the making and sipping of these special drinks. Stoke the fire, gather close together, and give a toast.

Pantry and Fridge Basics

Many of these ingredients are familiar staples you might already have on hand—but it never hurts to freshen up your stockpile with supplies especially for making cocktails. Once you've sampled a number of the recipes, you will have a handful of favorites and will always be ready to shake or stir something up.

Apple cider: This orchard elixir is the foundation for an assortment of beverages. Dense and cloudy, apple cider can be found at farmers' markets and in the refrigerated section of the supermarket. Do not substitute apple juice, which lacks cider's fresh intensity.

Bacon: Smoky, porky, satisfying: bacon has made its way into the cocktails arena as a spirit infusion and a garnish. Select high-quality, thick-cut bacon for more flavor and deeply satisfying bite.

Chiles: Fresh chiles, like the jalapeño and its extra-hot cousin the serrano, flavor tequila for intense Bloody Marías (page 95). Purchase chiles that are firm and smooth skinned; if you want a milder heat, remove and discard the seeds and ribs.

Chocolate: I always use bittersweet chocolate in my recipes, preferring the more intense flavor to that of milk chocolate. Look for varieties, either in bars or chips, that have 60 to 70 percent cacao. White chocolate is a chocolate derivative. During the manufacturing of chocolate, cacao bean solids are separated from the other components and later recombined. By contrast, these solids are left out of white chocolate, with the final product being made up of cocoa butter, milk, sugar, vanilla, and emulsifiers like lecithin. Be sure to purchase white chocolate that contains cocoa butter; inferior brands are often made with vegetable fat.

Club soda: This neutral, sparkling carbonated water adds fizz and balances out strong spirits without disturbing their flavors. Unless you plan to use a lot at once, such as in punches, keep small bottles on hand and store them in the fridge so you can add a splash here and there while preserving the carbonation.

Cocoa powder: After harvesting, cocoa beans are roasted. The shells and kernels (cocoa nibs) are separated, and the nibs are ground and heated to produce chocolate liquor. Next, cocoa butter is separated from the liquor, which results in natural cocoa powder. This variety is naturally acidic and the most commonly found in the United States. Dutch process cocoa is treated with an alkaline solution, which results in cocoa powder that is darker in color and mellower in flavor. In most cases, especially beverages, the two types are interchangeable; when baking, however, it is important to use the variety called for to avoid interfering with the success of chemical leaveners.

Coffee: Several recipes in this book are coffee based, such as Affogato Speciale (page 92). Use your favorite blend and, if possible, grind your beans for the freshest flavor. (A spice mill is perfect for small quantities.) French presses, stovetop espresso makers, and regular coffeepots are all acceptable for making coffee. Always brew coffee just before using it.

Dairy: Whole milk and heavy cream form the base for hot chocolates and are additions to smooth drinks like the White Russian (page 98).

Dried edible flowers: Dried lavender blossoms, chamomile, and rosebuds lend their fragrance to some of the lovelier drinks in this book. Some dried edible flowers are available at supermarkets; see Sources (page 138) for additional shopping suggestions.

Eggs: Every recipe in this book that relies on eggs, such as eggnog, calls for the large (not small, medium, extra-large, or jumbo) size. Prior to using, wash eggs to eliminate the risk of salmonella and let them come to room temperature for easier beating and incorporation.

Fresh herbs: Rosemary, thyme, and sage are frequently called for in the recipes in this book. To clean fresh herbs, fill a large bowl with cold water and soak them for a few minutes. Drain and repeat the process until the bottom of the bowl is free of sediment. Use herbs immediately or wrap leftovers in damp paper towels, place them in a plastic zip-top bag, and store them in the refrigerator's crisper drawer.

Fresh produce: Many of the recipes rely on seasonal produce. Apples, pears, pineapple, lemongrass and fresh ginger, and citrus fruits, such as oranges, Meyer lemons, and kumquats, are usually easy to find. Items like blood oranges may be more difficult to find out of season, so when they are available, snatch them up and try recipes that call for them. In many cases, citrus fruits are interchangeable.

Ginger beer: Ginger ale is one of the most refreshing carbonated beverages around, and I love the variety of craft versions, like Boylan's, that are available. However, I much prefer the sharper taste of ginger beer, whose more aggressive flavor is a refreshing and welcome addition to cocktails such as the Shandy (page 97).

Honey: Honey is a natural sweetener and a favorite in this book, especially in syrup form (page 108). I prefer dark and raw varieties; use your favorite.

Nuts: Whole hazelnuts, almonds, macadamia nuts, and pecans are featured in drink and snack recipes in this book. Nuts contain natural oils that can become rancid and damage flavor, so extend their shelf life by storing them in the freezer in airtight containers or plastic zip-top bags.

Peppercorns: Freshly ground black pepper is a must in any recipe that calls for it. Avoid ground varieties, which tend to lack flavor. Pink peppercorns, vaguely reminiscent of rose petals, add distinct flavor and gorgeous color. Keep them on hand for cocktails and for other recipes, such as cheese balls.

Salt: Kosher salt is the go-to in these recipes, but Maldon sea salt, which has large, flat crystals, is called on for garnishes. It melts slowly and evenly into warm foods and drinks and also provides a pleasant crunch when sprinkled on room-temperature or cold items.

Spices: Whole cloves, whole allspice, cinnamon sticks, whole nutmeg, black peppercorns, and pink peppercorns are crucial components of mulled drinks and garnishes. Spices lose potency with age, especially when stored in spaces that are constantly exposed to heat, such as cabinets above stovetops. Keep spices in a cool, dry area and avoid buying them in bulk so they don't go to waste. Many of the recipes in this book call for toasting spices in a dry skillet; this releases their flavor and makes it more discernible. Dry spices are often "bloomed," that is, briefly cooked in fat, to achieve the same effect. Most of the spices called for here are available at supermarkets, but see Sources (page 138) for harder-to-find items like Aleppo pepper.

Sugar: Granulated sugar, confectioners' or powdered sugar, and dark and light brown sugar are used in everything from Irish coffee to sangría. Keep several types on hand.

Sweetened condensed milk: You should always have this sweet treat in your pantry. It takes care of a sugar fix and also works as a quick dessert; a spoonful over chocolate ice cream is just the thing to end a meal. And it's essential for addictive drink recipes like Maríita's Alexander (page 76).

Tea: I like to make strong brews for tea-based drinks, so the recipes call for specific ratios of tea to water, but feel free to adjust them as you please. Chamomile and Earl Grey are absolutely necessary in the recipes that call for them and should not be substituted; hot toddy recipes can be flavored with your tea of choice. Loose leaf tea is preferred, but tea bags will usually do just as well. Although some loose-leaf teas will include brewing instructions, as a general rule you can start with a 6 to 8 ounces of freshly boiled water and 1 teaspoon of tea. Allow the tea to steep for 2 to 3 minutes, then strain and enjoy or cool as needed.

Tonic water: This carbonated soft drink contains quinine and is commonly used in cocktails like the classic gin and tonic. For purer flavor, I prefer brands that contain real quinine as opposed to flavorings and additives like corn syrup. Although not called for in this book, this basic cocktail mixer is great to have at the ready.

The Well-Stocked Bar

I usually drink my liquor straight and undiluted, sticking to good bourbon on the rocks or a very dirty (gin) martini, so my fridge and bar are always stocked with those spirits. I also have a handful of extra items on hand, such as Angostura bitters, St-Germain elderflower liqueur, and Kahlúa. I don't suggest you own every single spirit called for in this book, lest you want your home to look like a real bar, but I do recommend stocking your shelves with liquor that you drink often and the ingredients used in your favorite recipes. Remember, spirits have a long shelf life, so that bottle of crème de cassis that you use only once in a while will last until the next time you need a splash or two.

Aguardiente: Aguardiente literally means "burning water" in Spanish. It is a strong (29% or higher) spirit commonly distilled from fruits, grains, and sugarcane.

Amaretto: A sweet almond-flavored liqueur frequently served after dinner or combined with sour mix (try our homemade versions on page 110). It adds a mellow perfume to the Affogato Speciale (page 92).

Bährenjäger: This honey liqueur with a vodka base is produced in Germany. It's strong, sweet honey flavor is intense; a small amount goes a long way to flavor anything from champagne cocktails to the 1,001 Nights (page 51).

Beer: Bottled, canned, drafted: we all know beer. Varieties range from hopped-up India pale ales to hefty dark-brown stouts and seasonal craft varieties flavored with spices. Their flavors and consistencies vary almost infinitely. In this book, lagers as well as peach-flavored Belgian lambics are used to brew special potions (pages 92 and 97).

Bitters: Many types of these alcohols are infused with herbs, roots, citrus peel, seeds, flowers, and fruit, from the most recognizable Angostura to the most unusual plum bitters, which are heady and fruity. Bitters are added in dashes because the flavor is highly concentrated. Think of them as the salt that's added in pinches at the end of a recipe, to adjust seasoning.

Bourbon: An American whiskey, bourbon is distilled from a blend of grain that must contain no less than 51 percent corn. The remaining ingredients are usually barley, wheat, rye, or a combination thereof. The spirit is aged in flamed oak barrels, which lend a smoky, easily recognizable flavor. This is one of my favorite spirits and a potent potable: 80 percent alcohol content by volume.

Brandy: This spirit is distilled from wine. Note that cognac is brandy (named for the region of France in which it is produced), but not all brandy is Cognac. Brandies are often fruit flavored; some of these, such as pear-flavored brandy (also known as eau-de-vie), are used in this book (page 34).

Chambord: Syrupy and rich, this French raspberry liqueur is easily recognized by its distinctive round bottle and gold cap. A delicate splash is enough to flavor drinks like the Melba Shandy (page 97).

Champagne: Although the popular belief that French monk Dom Pérignon invented Champagne is untrue, the story about him exclaiming he'd tasted stars upon drinking it is one I'd like to believe. A sparkling white wine can only be called Champagne if made from grapes grown in that region of France. Always chill champagne prior to serving it. Champagne and sparkling wines should be stored at room temperature and chilled to about 45°F prior to serving. Place your bottle in the fridge about 6 hours before serving. Alternatively, fully submerge the bottle in an ice bucket and allow to rest for about 45 minutes. See page 21 for instructions on properly opening bottles.

Crème de cacao: This chocolate-flavored liqueur made from cacao beans is available in dark and clear varieties.

Crème de cassis: This is a black currant liqueur with a grape brandy or neutral spirit base. Sweet and dark red, it is a popular addition to cocktails, such as the kir royal and Classic Hot Chocolate (page 52).

Domaine de Canton: During France's colonization of southeast Asia, the French developed a taste for spiced and aromatic drafts. This liqueur is sharply flavored with fresh ginger and adds the right note to drinks like the Red Lipstick Margarita (page 91). Add a splash to simple cocktails like bourbon and ginger beer.

Gin: Bathtubs and the Prohibition era come to mind when I think of this spirit distilled from grain and herbs and spices, notably juniper berries. Long ago, it had medicinal purposes, but nowadays it is put to better use in cocktails. Make this clear, rather neutral spirit your own by flavoring it with infusions (pages 104 to 107).

Kahlúa: This coffee-flavored rum liqueur adds concentrated flavor and a hit of alcohol.

Port: This Portuguese fortified wine is known for its tawny hue. It is commonly consumed after dinner, and in this book it is served warm and spiced for a winter-perfect sip (see page 37).

Prosecco: Like champagne, prosecco is a sparkling white wine, but it hails from Italy rather than France. Keep bottles chilled and use them in punch recipes (starting on page 82).

Red wine: A discussion of wine could take up this entire book, so we'll focus only on those varieties called for in the recipes. Because the wines are mixed with other ingredients, select moderately priced bottles and opt for dry types like rioja, zinfandel, and cabernet sauvignon.

Rum: Yo, ho, ho. Rum is a spirit made by boiling sugarcane to thick molasses, which is later distilled and fermented. Dark rums are aged in oak barrels, which produce hues from sunset gold to dark mahogany. Their flavor is richer and more intense than those of light rums, which are not aged and thus have cleaner flavor but no color.

St-Germain: St-Germain is the original French elderflower liqueur. During a brief period, elderflowers are handpicked in the Alps and then used to produce this sweet, floral, delicate liqueur.

Tequila: This Mexican spirit is distilled from the blue agave plant, a succulent with fleshy, pointy leaves. The clear, young variety, known as white tequila, is often stirred into cocktails like the Margarita (page 90), whereas carefully aged versions, such as gold and *añejo* tequilas, are sipped straight. Tequila is complex and highly perfumed, but white varieties adapt well to flavoring agents like cilantro and chiles.

Vodka: The backbone of many cocktails in this book and beyond, this clear, practically odorless and clean-tasting, Russian-born spirit was originally distilled from potatoes; today's varieties contain other grains and sugars. Like gin, vodka is an ideal backdrop for infusions (pages 104 to 107), and often the two are used interchangeably in the recipes.

White wine: Just like its rosier counterpart, white wine will be addressed only briefly. Opt for moderately priced bottles and keep them chilled. Sweet white wines like riesling are the go-tos called for in this book.

A Guide to Tools and Serveware

Making a cocktail can be just as easy as pouring liquor into a clean glass (think whiskey neat), but for more elaborate mixes, a few tools are necessary. Following is a guide to tools and serveware that may prove useful in cocktail making.

Baking pans and metal mixing bowls: These are ideal for making large pieces of ice for chilling punches. A 13-by-9-inch baking pan is recommended for making treats like granitas.

Bar rags: Small, clean towels are perfect for cleaning up spills.

Bottle openers: Keep these around for popping open bottles of beer and carbonated beverages.

Chef's knife: For chopping and dicing ingredients, this utilitarian knife can't be beat.

Corkscrew: Although some wine bottles have screw tops, many a cork remains to be pulled.

Cutting boards: A small board is ideal for slicing citrus, chopping herbs, and prepping other ingredients and garnishes.

Fine-mesh sieve: For recipes that require ingredients to be strained, a fine-mesh sieve works best.

Ice bowl or bucket and tongs: Although not necessary, these two items add a nice touch to a bar.

Ice trays: I like to buy bags of ice for parties because it's convenient, but small pieces melt easily and water down drinks. Take the time to stock your freezer with homemade ice. Regular ice trays will do, or for a swankier presentation, try one of the specialty trays available. (See page 138 for Sources.)

Jigger: If you want to mix drinks properly, use a measure. Traditionally, a jigger is made of stainless steel and has an hourglass shape, with two different chambers for measuring liquids.

Muddler: This tool for smashing ingredients like fresh herbs, ginger, and sugar is often shaped like a baseball bat and has a fairly ergonomic design. In a pinch, substitute a wooden spoon.

Reamer or citrus juicer: These are efficient tools to get the most juice from citrus fruits. Reamers and citrus juicers are conical, with a pointy end and sharply grooved sides. Though juice can be extracted from citrus by simply cutting the fruit in half and squeezing with your hand, a reamer or juicer will yield more liquid. If you don't have either, use a fork.

Saucepans, large pots, and small skillets: Basic cookware is called for throughout this book for the making of syrups (pages 108 to 109), mulled ciders and wines (pages 33–39), and toasted spices (as on page 36). Stainless-steel pots are recommended for making caramel (page 20).

Shakers: There are three main types of cocktail shakers. All shakers are interchangeable; the type used is mostly a matter of personal preference. The *Boston shaker* consists of two parts: one stainless-steel cup and one glass or plastic pint cup. Ingredients are placed in the stainless-steel cup, and the other is fitted over it prior to shaking. The *cobbler shaker* has three pieces: a stainless-steel cup, a built-in strainer, and a lid. The *French shaker* is a two-piece construction with a metal bottom and cap; a strainer is needed for serving.

Sealable glass bottles and jars: When sterilized these are ideal for prepping and storing beverages ahead of time.

Stirrers or swizzle sticks: These long-necked spoons are useful for blending drinks in tall glasses.

Strainer: Bar strainers are small and fit the mouths of shaker cups. Several chilled drinks (pages 76–99) in this book contain ingredients and ice that need to be strained and discarded prior to pouring and serving.

Know Your Glassware

When making cocktails, I prefer to take the fuss out of serving. I pour drinks into whatever glasses are available and serve mixtures like punch in anything that will hold large amounts of liquid. But it's nice to know that there are specific vessels designed for specific drinks. The key is to make sure that the capacity of the glass can accommodate the beverage you're serving.

Champagne glasses: Narrow flutes are slim and tall and allow you to see the lovely characteristic bubbles of sparkling wine. Marie Antoinette–style or birdbath-style glasses have wide, shallow bowls sitting atop delicate stems.

Cocktail or martini glasses: These have thin stems with conical bowls. Modern versions are sometimes available stemless.

Collins glasses: Tall and slim, these glasses usually hold 10 to 12 ounces.

Highball glasses: These tall tumblers are somewhat wider and shorter than collins glasses. Capacity is normally 8 to 12 ounces.

Irish coffee glasses: These are footed mugs with handles that are heat resistant, making them perfect for serving mulled drinks and other warm beverages. Capacity ranges from 8 to 12 ounces.

Mugs: Mugs are sturdy, heavy vessels designed with a comfortably large handle. Their thickness retains heat, especially when the mugs are prewarmed, and their capacity to hold more liquid than teacups and espresso cups makes them perfect for hot beverages like American coffee and Hot Chocolates (pages 52–56).

Old-fashioned glasses: Also known as lowball or rocks glasses, these short, squat, thick-based tumblers hold 5 to 10 ounces and are used to serve specific cocktails like the classic Old Fashioned (whence the name comes) and Black and White Russians (page 98).

Shot glasses: These short, footless glasses typically hold 1½ ounces, though some are available in 1- or 2-ounce capacities. They are ideal for shooting spirits or, in a bind, good for measuring liquid ingredients in cocktails.

Wineglasses: These come in different stem heights and bowl sizes and shapes; each is specific to the type of wine being served. Stemless glasses are a great option for chilled drinks in this book (pages 93–116).

Some Like It Hot, Some Like It Cold

A nice touch when making heated drinks is to serve them in warm containers, the better to maintain their temperature. Run cups under hot tap water for a minute or two, dry thoroughly, and keep them in a warm place covered with a towel until time to serve. Chill glasses for cold drinks by placing them on a tray in the refrigerator or freezing them for 5 minutes prior to serving.

Do It This Way

CRUSH IT.

Muddling

Muddling is a technique used to release ingredients' flavors. Herbs and other items such as fresh ginger and lemongrass are placed in a cocktail shaker and gently crushed, often with abrasives like sugar or salt to aid in breaking down. Do not overwork the ingredients, especially herbs; a soft bruising is all they need to release their natural oils and flavors. Muddlers are specifically designed for comfortable and efficient work; however, the back of a wooden cooking spoon is an apt substitute.

Step 1

Place ingredients to be muddled in a cocktail shaker or glass.

Step 2

Gently press ingredients down against sides of the cocktail shaker or glass until herbs are slightly bruised and any fruits are smashed.

Step 3

Add liquids and ice per recipe. If called for, shake mixture and strain into glass. Discard solids.

Flavored Rims

Flavored rims add an extra flavor to drinks. A glass rim is moistened with an ingredient and then dipped into a dry flavoring agent, such as salt. Gussy up rims with spices and crushed herbs. You can moisten the rims with ingredients included in the cocktail you're preparing, such as citrus juices and liqueurs, or with complementary liquid flavoring agents. I like a rim moistened with hot sauce in a Bloody Mary (pages 94-95) or a sugar and crushed cilantro rim for the Margarita (pages 90-91).

Step 1

Wet the rim of a glass or cup with a flavored spirit or citrus juice.

Step 2

Place sugar, salt, or other dry flavoring on a small plate.

Step 3

Dip rim of glass in the dry flavoring and shake off excess. Proceed with recipe.

DARK AND INTENSE.

Caramel

Caramel is produced when sugar is cooked to a dark amber color. Though the process is easy, it does require careful attention—there is a fine line between caramel and burnt sugar. Use a stainless-steel pot, removing it from the heat as soon as a slender wisp of smoke rises. Freshly caramelized sugar is bolder and more deeply flavored than cloying commercial versions. It adds a strong, smoky backdrop to drinks like the Burnt-Sugar Hot Buttered Rum (page 30).

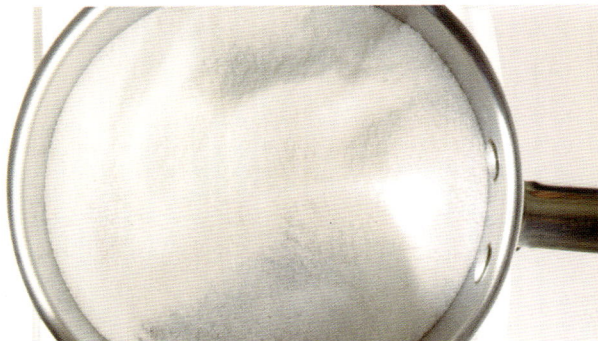

Step 1

Place sugar and water in a deep, stainless-steel saucepan.

Step 2

Cook over medium-high heat, swirling—but not stirring—the pan occasionally to keep the sugar at the bottom of the pan, rather than up the sides.

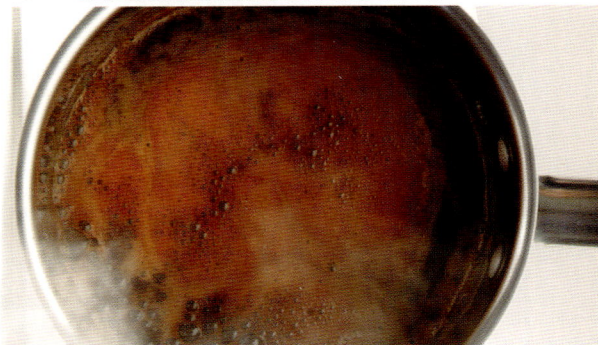

Step 3

Remove the pan from the heat as soon as the caramel turns dark amber and just begins to smoke.

Opening Champagne

A saber is not always handy, so most of us will have to rely on our two hands to open bottles of bubbly. Although it's quite festive to pop a cork and allow a shower of effervescent liquid to spill out, the goal is to keep as much of the champagne in the bottle so that you can actually drink it. Always chill champagne thoroughly before serving.

Remove the foil wrapper.

Unwind the wire cage and remove it.

Make sure no guests or valuables are within close range. Hold the cork with one hand and, with the other, grasp the bottle at the point where the neck tapers. Twist the bottle, *not* the cork. Six to seven twists should do it, and then . . . *pop!*

Citrus Garnishes

Popular cocktail garnishes, citrus peels provide a decorative touch while enhancing flavor and aroma. Simple slices are common, as are thick peels. Select fruits with unblemished skins and gently pick out any seeds. Blood oranges, tangerines, Meyer lemons, grapefruits, kumquats—try whatever is in season where you live.

Step 1

Use a sharp vegetable peeler or channel knife to remove the skin; avoid the white pith.

Step 2

Wrap the peel or zest around a straw or chopstick to help shape it into a curl.

Step 3

Release extra flavor by carefully running a flame on the zest. Rub the rim of the glass to add a note of fragrance.

Granita

For these easy-to-make shaved ices, all you need to do is scrape the flavored ice with a fork every hour or so, until the mixture is completely frozen. Granitas are a simple dessert that originated in Sicily. The wonderful thing is that you can make them with essentially any flavor combinations, and, more important, you don't need an ice cream machine. I like to experiment with surprising combinations, such as watermelon-chili and melon-honey-peppercorn.

Pour flavored mixture into a large freezer-safe bowl or 13-by-9-inch baking pan.

Scrape with the tines of a fork about every 30 minutes until mixture is frozen.

Granita is ready when it is completely frozen and has a finely shaved texture.

Hot Toddies and Mulled Drinks

ORANGES
2 BOTTLES WHITE WINE
APPLE CIDER
SUGAR
CINNAMON STICKS
MILK
COFFEE
BRANDY
RUM
APPLES
GIN

Hot Toddies and Mulled Drinks have been served for centuries, and for good reason: they warm the body and soothe the mind. Settle down to watch a snowstorm howl with a steaming Hot Toddy, make multiple batches of Mulled White Wine and ladle cupfuls to guests when they arrive at your next wintry gathering, or skip dessert and spoon a mound of freshly whipped cream on top of a spiked cider.

What's cooking? From left to right: Hot Toddy, Mulled Wine, Mulled White Wine, and boiled water on standby.

Hot Toddy

SERVES 4

In times past, hot toddies were often prescribed as a head-cold remedy. Today, liquor as medication is generally frowned upon because of its dehydrating effects. However, if you're one of those people who can't tolerate over-the-counter pharmaceuticals, this beverage may offer the relief you need—just drink an extra glass of water to replenish your body.

6 tablespoons honey

8 ounces bourbon, rye whiskey, or dark rum

24 ounces boiling water

4 lemon slices

Pour 1½ tablespoons honey in each of 4 warmed cups. Add bourbon, rye, or rum and then water. Stir until honey is completely dissolved. Garnish each cup with a lemon slice and serve.

OTHER CUDDLE-WORTHY TODDIES

Gin Toddy
Substitute **Kumquat-Thyme Infused Gin** (page 106) or **Chamomile-Pear Infused Gin** (page 106) for the bourbon.

Applejack Toddy
Substitute **pure maple syrup** for the honey and **applejack** for the bourbon. **Cinnamon tea** may be substituted for the boiling water.

More to Try
You can make a toddy with whatever flavor you please—it's a good way to use infused liquors (see page 104). These drinks can be flavored further by substituting hot tea for the boiling water.

Pair Hot Toddies with easy-to-make Cheater Doughnuts rolled in Spicy Sage Sugar or dunked in a variety of homemade glazes (pages 126-128).

Hot Buttered Rum

This drink requires little explanation: it's hot rum served with a pat of butter. Sometimes spices, sweeteners, and water are added to the mix. The butter may sound like an odd addition, but it brings a silky quality to the drink. In this version, the butter is flavored with vanilla bean seeds and dark brown sugar for a well-rounded drink.

Drinks

6 ounces dark rum

3 cups hot water

Vanilla Bean Butter

4 tablespoons unsalted butter, at room temperature

1 vanilla bean pod, seeds scraped out, pods reserved for different use

1½ tablespoons packed dark brown sugar

Pinch salt

Pinch ground cinnamon

Pinch ground mace

For the drinks: Stir together rum and water. Place 1 tablespoon Vanilla Bean Butter in each of 4 warmed cups. Pour rum into cups. Serve.

For the Vanilla Bean Butter: Vigorously mix ingredients together in a medium bowl. Set aside until ready to use. If making in advance, store in a small bowl wrapped in plastic, refrigerate, and then return to room temperature before using.

AN EVEN SWEETER VERSION

Burnt-Sugar Hot Buttered Rum

Stir together ¾ **cup granulated sugar** and ¼ **cup water** in a large heavy-bottomed saucepan over medium-high heat. Cook, swirling pan occasionally, until mixture turns dark amber and just begins to smoke, 6 to 8 minutes. Immediately add **3 cups water**, stepping away from the pan until bubbling and sputtering subside. Reduce heat to medium and stir just until mixture is smooth. Stir in rum and proceed with recipe as above.

Vanilla Bean Butter is delicious in Hot Buttered Rum and just as good on toast. Double the recipe so there's plenty extra for snacking.

Mulled Wine

This warm drink is made with red wine and a blend of spices that infuse it with warmth and fragrance. Mulling refers to the process of heating a liquid, most notably an alcoholic one such as wine, with flavoring agents such as sweeteners and spices. Since the wine will be flavored, use an affordable variety rather than a special vintage. Often, mulled wines are sweetened and enhanced with fresh and dried fruits, as in this recipe.

1 tablespoon green cardamom pods, crushed*

1 tablespoon black peppercorns

2 teaspoons whole cloves

3 cinnamon sticks

1 (750-milliliter) bottle dry red wine, such as Côtes du Rhône

1 cup brandy

Rind and 2 tablespoons juice from 1 lemon

⅓ cup honey

1 Bosc pear, peeled, cored, and cut into ¼-inch dice

*To crush the pods, use the back of a chef's knife or smooth side of a meat mallet and press down. Normally, the black seeds are picked out and the shells discarded. In this recipe, however, the cardamom will be strained out, so the entire crushed pod can be added, shell and all.

This recipe calls for lemon rind and juice, but you can use orange, clementine, kumquat, or any other fresh citrus you like.

Place cardamom, peppercorns, cloves, and cinnamon in a medium saucepan. Stir over medium heat until fragrant, about 2 minutes. Add wine, brandy, lemon rind and juice, and honey and bring to a simmer over medium heat, stirring occasionally. Reduce heat to lowest setting and simmer for 10 minutes.

Strain mixture through a fine-mesh sieve into a bowl and discard solids. Return mixture to saucepan and add pears. Simmer over medium-low heat until pears are fork-tender but still retain their shape, about 10 minutes. Serve.

The More, the Merrier

Mulled Wine can be easily multiplied and served to a crowd. Prepare the recipe in a large pot or Dutch oven instead of a medium saucepan. Serve it straight out of the pot, pouring servings into heatproof cups.

Mulled White Wine

Fruity white zinfandel gets a boozy boost from pear eau-de-vie and fresh lemony and floral flavor from sage and thyme. It's less expected but just as warming as its traditional red counterpart.

2 teaspoons black peppercorns

2 teaspoons whole cloves

1 (750-milliliter) bottle white zinfandel

¼ cup granulated sugar

1 small bunch sage

1 small bunch thyme

Rind and 2 tablespoons juice from 1 lemon

1 cup pear eau-de-vie or brandy

1 firm, ripe pear,* peeled, cored, and thinly sliced

Any pear will do, but Forelle, a petite and dainty variety, makes for a lovely presentation.

Place peppercorns and cloves in a medium saucepan. Stir over medium heat until fragrant, about 2 minutes. Add wine, sugar, sage, thyme, and lemon rind and juice and bring to a simmer over medium heat, stirring until sugar is completely dissolved. Reduce heat to lowest setting and simmer for 10 minutes.

Strain mixture through a fine-mesh sieve into a bowl and discard solids. Return mixture to saucepan and stir in eau-de-vie and pear slices. Simmer over medium-low heat until pears are fork-tender but still retain their shape, 8 to 10 minutes. Serve.

Let No One Go Thirsty

Mulled White Wine can be easily multiplied and served to a crowd. Prepare the recipe in a large pot or Dutch oven instead of a medium saucepan. Serve it straight out of the pot, pouring servings into heatproof cups.

For a more decorative touch, leave the skin, seeds, and stems on the pears.

Eve's Addiction

• SERVES 4 •

When we begin to hide from the brusque snap of cold weather, there is no better comfort than a hot drink that brings a tingling sensation to the fingertips and then washes over us with warmth. Apple cider, ruddy and cloudy, is best served heated with additional fiery flavor from spices and, of course, a splash of spirits. Tart apple bits, dried cranberries, and clementine slices enhance this classic.

In addition to the expected cloves and allspice, this cider includes black peppercorns for a subtle burn and coriander for its notes of citrus. For an extra treat, top it with freshly whipped cream (see **Irish Coffee**, page 68).

1 tablespoon whole allspice berries

1 tablespoon black peppercorns

1 tablespoon whole cloves

2 teaspoons whole coriander

3 cinnamon sticks

4 ½ cups apple cider

Rind and ¼ cup juice from 1 large orange

8 ounces applejack

1 Granny Smith apple, peeled, cored, and cut into ¼-inch slices

1 clementine or small orange, scrubbed and cut into ¼-inch-thick rounds

2 tablespoons dried cranberries

Place allspice, peppercorns, cloves, coriander, and cinnamon in a medium saucepan. Cook, stirring, over medium heat until fragrant, about 2 minutes. Stir in apple cider, orange rind and juice, and applejack and bring to a simmer over medium heat, stirring occasionally. Reduce heat to lowest setting and simmer for 15 minutes.

Strain mixture through a fine-mesh sieve into a bowl and discard solids. Return cider to saucepan and add apples, clementines, and cranberries. Simmer over medium-low heat until apples are fork-tender but still retain their shape and cranberries are plump, about 10 minutes. Serve.

Roll Out the Barrels

Eve's Addiction and its variations can be easily multiplied and served to a crowd. Prepare the recipe in a large pot or Dutch oven instead of a medium saucepan. Serve it straight out of the pot, pouring servings into heatproof cups.

TWO MORE BLENDS TO TRY

Red Riding Hood

A simple twist on the previous mulled cider recipe, this version is just as boldly spiced but has a ruby tint and added depth thanks to the red wine. Omit the applejack and combine **3 cups apple cider** and **1½ cups dry red wine** with the orange rind and juice after toasting the spices.

Tart and Tawny

Tart, crimson cranberry juice is frequently paired with apple cider. Here, port joins the duo: sweet, smooth, and tawny, it curbs the bitterness of the berry juice and makes it much more enticing. Follow the base recipe but omit the applejack and combine **3 cups cranberry juice**, **1 cup apple cider**, and **8 ounces tawny port** after toasting the spices.

Liquid Gold

SERVES 4

Though it calls to mind a tropical setting, the pineapple is in fact a winter fruit. It is also an iconic symbol of hospitality. Warm your home and your friends with this mulled pineapple drink that showcases both its sweet and tart flavors.

Pineapple Garnish

12 or more (¾-inch) cubes fresh pineapple

1 tablespoon granulated sugar

¼ teaspoon Aleppo pepper*

¼ teaspoon ground cinnamon

⅛ teaspoon salt

Mulled Pineapple Juice

1 tablespoon whole allspice berries

1 tablespoon black peppercorns

1 tablespoon whole cloves

2 cinnamon sticks

4 cups pineapple juice

6 ounces dark rum

2 ounces brandy

1 vanilla bean pod, split in half lengthwise, seeds scraped out

*Piquant and vibrant, Aleppo is a type of crushed red pepper native to Syria. It is available at specialty markets (see Sources, page 138).

For the Pineapple Garnish: Adjust an oven rack to the middle position and preheat broiler. Line a baking sheet with foil and arrange pineapple cubes in a single layer. Combine sugar, Aleppo pepper, ground cinnamon, and salt in a small bowl. Sprinkle pineapple cubes with sugar mixture and toss to coat evenly. Rearrange pineapple in a single layer and broil until caramelized, 2 to 4 minutes. Transfer tray to cooling rack. When cool enough to handle, skewer at least 3 pineapple cubes onto each of 4 short skewers or sturdy toothpicks (see page 138 for Sources).

For the Mulled Pineapple Juice: Place allspice, peppercorns, cloves, and cinnamon sticks in a medium saucepan. Stir over medium heat until fragrant, about 2 minutes. Add pineapple juice, rum, brandy, and vanilla bean and seeds and bring to a simmer over medium heat, stirring occasionally. Reduce heat to lowest setting and simmer for 15 minutes.

Strain mixture through a fine-mesh sieve into a bowl and discard solids. To serve, place one pineapple skewer in each of 4 heat-proof cups. Ladle juice into cups.

Eggnog, Hot Chocolate, Coffee, and Tea

Velvety whipped eggnogs, thick hot chocolates (both dark and white varieties), intense black-coffee drinks, and soothing teas are all about comfort and joy. Work your way through these warm and easily spike-able drinks as the cold months wear on. The recipes for Classic Eggnog and its variations will bring it back in vogue during the holiday season, White Hot Chocolate with macadamia nuts and pink peppercorns will definitely put that to-go version to shame, and tea will go from *Zzzzz* to *Kapow!*

Warm up with concoctions like (from left to right) Classic Hot Chocolate, Butterscotch Eggnog, The English Rose, Mama's Remedy, and Irish Coffee.

Classic Eggnog

MAKES ABOUT 2 QUARTS (12 TO 14 SERVINGS)

Eggnog is a milk- or cream-based beverage sweetened with sugar and spiked with spirits such as rum, brandy, whiskey, or a combination thereof. Eggs, of course, are the main ingredient—and are responsible for the drink's shady reputation for harboring germs. However, fresh eggs are unlikely to cause salmonella infection or other bacteria-bred illnesses. And since eggs give eggnog its characteristic velvety texture and cloudlike froth—the yolks build the custardy base, and the whites add lightness—there are no substitutions. If you're concerned about bacteria, wash the eggs before using them because any bacteria would come from the shell.

8 large eggs,* separated
¼ cup packed dark brown sugar
Pinch salt
2 cups heavy cream
2 cups whole milk
1 cup brandy**
1 cup dark rum
1 tablespoon pure vanilla extract
½ cup granulated sugar
Freshly grated nutmeg

*Eggs are more easily beaten and incorporated into recipes when they are at room temperature. Either let them sit at room temperature for at least an hour, or soak them in warm tap water for about 10 minutes.

**All eggnog recipes may be made without alcohol.

In a large bowl, whisk egg yolks, brown sugar, and salt until thickened and pale brown in color, 2 to 3 minutes. Whisk in cream and milk, followed by the brandy, rum, and vanilla.

In a separate large, clean bowl, whip egg whites with an electric mixer on medium speed until soft peaks form, about 2 minutes. Gradually add granulated sugar and continue whipping until firm, glossy peaks form, 1 to 2 minutes longer (see page 68 for more on whipping cream).

Transfer cream mixture to a punch or serving bowl. Fold in egg whites with a rubber spatula and ladle portions into cups. Sprinkle with freshly grated nutmeg and serve.

Pumpkin-Bourbon Eggnog

MAKES ABOUT 2 QUARTS (12 TO 14 SERVINGS)

This eggnog variation goes hand-in-glove with the coming of the colder months and holiday festivities. Pumpkin puree, brown sugar, and spices blend with milk, cream, and bourbon for a drink that rivals dessert.

2 tablespoons unsalted butter

1 cup pumpkin puree

1 ½ teaspoons ground cinnamon, plus more for sprinkling

½ teaspoon ground allspice

Pinch salt

2 cups heavy cream

2 cups whole milk

1 ½ cups bourbon

½ cup brandy or cognac

8 large eggs, separated

¼ cup packed dark brown sugar

2 teaspoons pure vanilla extract

½ cup granulated sugar

Melt butter over medium heat in a medium saucepan. Add pumpkin, cinnamon, allspice, and salt and cook, stirring, for 2 minutes. Whisk in cream, milk, bourbon, and brandy or cognac and bring to a simmer. Remove from heat and cover to keep warm.

In a large bowl, whisk egg yolks, brown sugar, and vanilla until thickened (wrap a damp kitchen towel around the base of the bowl to keep it steady while you whisk). Pour the pumpkin mixture into the egg yolk mixture, whisking constantly until well incorporated. Pour mixture back into saucepan and cover to keep warm.

In a separate large bowl whip egg whites with an electric mixer on medium speed until soft peaks form, about 2 minutes. Gradually add granulated sugar and continue whipping until firm, glossy peaks form, 1 to 2 minutes longer.

Transfer cream mixture to a punch or serving bowl. Fold in egg whites with a rubber spatula and ladle portions into warmed heatproof glasses or mugs. If serving cold, allow the pumpkin base to cool to room temperature and then refrigerate until well chilled. Fold in egg whites and ladle into chilled glasses.

Butterscotch Eggnog

MAKES ABOUT 2 QUARTS (12 TO 14 SERVINGS)

Notes of burnt caramel melt into this eggnog variation that is wonderful served warm or chilled. Large, crisp flakes of Maldon salt float on the frothy surface for textural contrast and a flavor that highlights the butterscotch.

2 cups heavy cream

2 cups whole milk

½ cup water

1½ cups granulated sugar, divided

8 large eggs, separated

¼ cup packed dark brown sugar

2 teaspoons pure vanilla extract

2 cups bourbon

Maldon salt, for garnish

Cooking Tip

Making caramel may seem daunting, all that is required is careful attention. Be prepared for the moment the caramel begins to turn dark amber and gently smoke: immediately add the cream and milk to prevent it from burning. (See page 20 for a step-by-step photographic how-to.)

Combine cream and milk in a bowl or measuring cup. Stir together water with 1 cup of the sugar in a large, heavy-bottom saucepan over medium-high heat. Cook, swirling pan occasionally, until sugar turns dark amber and just begins to smoke, 6 to 8 minutes. Immediately add cream mixture, stepping away from pan until bubbling and sputtering subside. Reduce heat to medium and stir just until mixture is smooth. Remove from heat.

In a large bowl, whisk egg yolks, brown sugar, and vanilla until thickened (wrap a damp kitchen towel around the base of the bowl to keep it steady while you whisk). Whisking constantly, pour the caramel mixture into the egg yolk mixture and combine until well incorporated. Whisk in bourbon. Pour mixture back into saucepan and cover to keep warm.

In a separate large bowl whip egg whites with an electric mixer on medium speed until soft peaks form, about 2 minutes. Gradually add the remaining 1 cup granulated sugar and continue whipping until firm, glossy peaks form, 1 to 2 minutes longer.

Transfer cream mixture to a punch or serving bowl. Fold in egg whites with a rubber spatula and ladle portions into warmed heatproof glasses or mugs. If serving cold, allow the pumpkin mixture to cool to room temperature, then refrigerate until well chilled. Fold in egg whites and ladle portions into chilled glasses. Sprinkle with Maldon salt before serving.

Rompope

SERVES 6 TO 8

The first *rompope*, a derivation of Spanish *ponche de huevo* (egg punch), was brewed by seventeenth-century nuns in the Santa Clara convent in Puebla, Mexico. According to legend, Sister Eduviges requested that the nuns be allowed to drink the rompope they were only permitted to make. Legend also has it that there was one secret ingredient in the recipe that Eduviges took with her to the grave.

Rompope is served chilled, often over ice, but it can be served warm, which is how I prefer it when cold weather sets in. Either way, it's rich, velvety, fragrant, and certainly full of cheer.

⅔ cup blanched almonds

1½ cups plus 2 tablespoons granulated sugar, divided

6 cups whole milk

2 cinnamon sticks

Rind of 1 lemon*

1 teaspoon pure vanilla extract

¼ teaspoon baking soda

8 large egg yolks

1 cup white rum or *aguardiente***

Remove the lemon rind with a vegetable peeler, being careful to avoid the white pith, which will impart a bitter flavor.

**Aguardiente *literally means "burning water" in Spanish. It is a strong (29% or higher) spirit distilled from fruits, grains, and commonly sugarcane. It's available at most liquor stores; for additional sources, see page 138.*

Pulse almonds with 2 tablespoons of the sugar in a food processor until ground to a fine paste.

Bring milk, cinnamon, lemon rind, vanilla, and baking soda to a boil over medium-high heat in a large heavy-bottom saucepan. Reduce heat to medium-low and simmer for 15 to 20 minutes. Set aside.

In a large bowl, whisk egg yolks, the remaining 1½ cups sugar, and ground almonds until thick and pale. Remove cinnamon and lemon rind and discard. Whisking constantly, slowly add the milk to the yolk mixture.

Return mixture to pan and cook over low heat, constantly stirring and scraping the bottom and sides of the pan, until the mixture thickens enough to coat the back of a spoon, 5 to 7 minutes. Set aside to cool completely, about 2 hours.

Stir in rum or *aguardiente*. Serve.

Make-Ahead Tip

Rompope may be refrigerated for up to one month in sterilized glass bottles.

Bottled Coquito (page 50) and glasses of Rompope are Puerto Rican and Mexican milk punches.

Coquito

SERVES 8 TO 10

Coquito brings a refreshing and tropical twist to the winter season. Like rompope, it is traditionally poured and shared on *nochebuena* (Christmas Eve) and given out as a gift in festively wrapped bottles, but it will fit in at any holiday celebration. The recipe is similar to rompope, but with a few tweaks: sweetened condensed milk acts as a sweetener, evaporated milk takes the place of milk, and, of course, the island influence is asserted with coconut milk and rum. (For a photo of this drink, see page 49.)

1 (12-ounce) can evaporated milk

8 whole cloves

1 cinnamon stick

1 (2-inch) piece ginger, peeled and cut crosswise into thin rounds

1 (15-ounce) can sweetened condensed milk

1 (13.5-ounce) can coconut milk*

1 cup white rum

4 large egg yolks

2 teaspoons pure vanilla extract

¼ teaspoon ground cinnamon, plus more for garnish

⅛ teaspoon freshly ground nutmeg, plus more for garnish

Do not substitute cream of coconut for the coconut milk, because the drink will be too sweet.

Bring evaporated milk, cloves, cinnamon, and ginger to a boil over medium-high heat in a small saucepan. Remove from heat and let steep for 30 minutes. Strain liquid through a fine-mesh sieve and discard solids. Let cool to room temperature, about 20 minutes.

Place spiced milk mixture, sweetened condensed milk, coconut milk, rum, egg yolks, vanilla, ground cinnamon, and nutmeg in a blender and blend until fully combined and foamy, 1 to 2 minutes.

Pour into chilled glasses and dust with additional cinnamon and nutmeg.

1,001 Nights

Dates evoke exotic stories of velvet nights studded with a million glittering stars. This sweet drink would have soothed even Scheherazade's fitful king.

1½ cups dark rum

1 cup dates, pitted and chopped

2 cinnamon sticks

4 cups (32 ounces) coconut milk

Pinch salt

3 tablespoons honey

1 cup heavy cream, chilled

¼ cup confectioners' sugar

1 ounce Bährenjäger honey liqueur

1 cup **Whipped Cream** (page 68), or more if desired, for garnish

Toasted coconut flakes,* for garnish

To toast coconut flakes, arrange them in a single layer on a rimmed baking sheet and bake in a preheated 350°F oven for 7 to 10 minutes, stirring halfway through baking, until toasted. Alternatively, toast them in a large dry skillet over medium heat, stirring occasionally, until golden, 5 to 7 minutes.

Bring rum, dates, and cinnamon to a simmer in a medium saucepan over medium heat. Reduce heat to low and simmer until dates are plump and soft and most of the liquid has been absorbed, about 8 minutes. Remove from heat and let cool for 5 minutes.

Transfer mixture to a blender. Add coconut milk and salt and pulse until pureed. Return mixture to saucepan and simmer over low heat until heated through, about 5 minutes. Add honey and stir until incorporated. Remove from heat and strain through a fine-mesh sieve into a large bowl, discarding solids.

Using an electric mixer, beat heavy cream, confectioners' sugar, and honey liqueur on medium speed in a large, chilled bowl until soft peaks form, 2 to 3 minutes. (Alternatively, beat by hand using a large wire whisk.) Ladle drink into warm cups, top with whipped cream, and sprinkle with toasted coconut flakes.

Classic Hot Chocolate

SERVES 4

A potent cup of coffee, well-brewed and aromatic, is instantly electrifying and just the thing for an on-the-go afternoon, but when the pace is leisurely and the dusk is rubbing shoulders with the chill, a rich cup of hot chocolate is a better potion.

Instead of those pale brown and dusty single-serve packets that deliver a weak and watery sip, try this luxurious version that combines cocoa powder and bittersweet chocolate. This drinking chocolate is meant to be rich and thick, but it can be thinned out to taste by adding a bit more milk.

4 tablespoons (½ stick) unsalted butter

½ cup natural cocoa powder*

3 tablespoons packed dark brown sugar

4 cups whole milk

6 ounces finely chopped bittersweet chocolate** or bittersweet chocolate chips

Pinch salt

1 tablespoon pure vanilla extract

6 ounces Chambord or crème de cassis, optional

8 **Homemade Marshmallows** (page 116) or **Whipped Cream** (page 68), for serving

See page 12 for how natural cocoa powder differs from Dutch process.

Melt butter in a medium saucepan over medium heat. Add cocoa powder and brown sugar and whisk until a paste forms. Slowly add milk, whisking constantly. Bring to a simmer over medium-high heat and then reduce heat to medium-low. Stir in chocolate and salt and cook, stirring, until chocolate is completely melted. Remove from heat and stir in vanilla.

Serve in warm mugs and spike with 1½ ounces Chambord or crème de cassis per serving, if desired. Top with marshmallows or whipped cream.

In Full Bloom

Cocoa powder, as well as ground dry spices, is more flavorful when "bloomed," or quickly cooked in fat—in this case, butter—prior to being incorporated into the recipe.

Cherry-Vanilla Hot Chocolate

To make this variation of **Classic Hot Chocolate**, replace the brown sugar with ¼ **cup granulated sugar into which the seeds of 1 vanilla bean pod*** have been rubbed. Substitute **4 ounces high-quality white chocolate** for 4 ounces of the bittersweet chocolate. Instead of Chambord or crème de cassis, spike with **1½ ounces kirsch (cherry liqueur)** per serving.

Whole vanilla bean pods should have the texture of soft leather. Use a paring knife to slit the pod in half lengthwise and then run the dull edge of the knife down along the inside of the pod to scrape out the seeds. Recycle the scraped pods by storing them in sugar used for coffee or tea: the sugar will acquire a gentle taste of vanilla.

To the Bitter End

Bittersweet chocolate, which contains 60 to 70 percent cacao solids, produces the most boldly flavored hot chocolate. Brands such as Ghirardelli or Scharffen Berger are recommended.

Earl Grey–Lavender Hot Chocolate

Some flavors, like cinnamon and sugar, are obvious pairings, whereas others are less so. If you venture out a bit, you'll find that more unusual combinations make just as much sense, as in this recipe: staid Earl Grey tea meets gentle lavender, and both flavors sink gently into simmering chocolate.

½ cup dried edible lavender flowers (see page 138 for Sources)

½ cup loose Earl Grey tea

4 cups whole milk

4 tablespoons (½ stick) unsalted butter

½ cup natural cocoa powder

3 tablespoons packed dark brown sugar

6 ounces finely chopped bittersweet chocolate or bittersweet chocolate chips

Pinch salt

1 tablespoon pure vanilla extract

6 ounces Bährenjäger honey liqueur,* optional

*Bährenjäger is a honey liqueur that stands in for honey here, doing double duty as sweetener and spiking agent.

Bring lavender, tea, and milk to a simmer in a medium, heavy-bottomed saucepan over medium heat, stirring occasionally. Remove from heat and let steep for 15 minutes. Strain mixture through a fine-mesh sieve into a bowl and discard solids. Wipe out saucepan.

In the same pan, melt butter over medium heat. Add cocoa powder and brown sugar and whisk together until a paste forms. Slowly add milk, whisking constantly. Bring to a simmer over medium-high heat and reduce heat to medium-low. Stir in chocolate and salt and cook, stirring, until chocolate is completely melted.

Serve and spike with 1½ ounces Bährenjäger per serving, if desired.

Winter White Hot Chocolate

SERVES 4

White chocolate replaces bittersweet in this version of the cold-weather favorite. The satiny blend of milk and creamy white chocolate is luxe on its own, but it melds effortlessly with unique ingredients like almond extract—and spirits, of course. Lemon juice and salt balance the flavors of this rich, velvety drink.

4 cups whole milk

6 ounces white chocolate,* finely chopped

Pinch salt

1 teaspoon pure almond extract

1 teaspoon pure vanilla extract

2 teaspoons fresh lemon juice

Use the best-quality white chocolate you can find (Callebaut or Cadbury are highly recommended brands). Lower grade varieties tend to be chalky and overly sweet.

Bring milk to a simmer in a medium saucepan over medium-high heat and then reduce heat to medium-low. Stir in white chocolate and salt and cook, stirring, until chocolate is completely melted. Remove from heat and stir in vanilla and almond extracts and lemon juice. Serve in warmed cups.

A BRACING ALTERNATIVE

Minty Winter White Hot Chocolate

For a cool twist, omit the almond extract and spike drinks with **1½ ounces peppermint schnapps** per serving.

Salted Caramel Hot Chocolate

In this version of **Classic Hot Chocolate** (page 52), dark chocolate acquires a bold sidekick: salted caramel, which adds complementary bittersweet notes. Both flavors are accentuated with a sprinkling of flaky sea salt.

1½ cups granulated sugar

¾ cup water

6 tablespoons light corn syrup

1 cup heavy cream

1 teaspoon Maldon salt, plus more for garnish*

4 tablespoons (½ stick) unsalted butter

½ cup natural cocoa powder

3 tablespoons packed dark brown sugar

4 cups whole milk

6 ounces finely chopped bittersweet chocolate or bittersweet chocolate chips

2 teaspoons pure vanilla extract

6 ounces amaretto, optional

Maldon salt is a sea salt whose large flakes are ideal for seasoning: they melt slowly into warm items and provide a nice crunch and textural contrast. See page 138 for Sources.

Stir sugar, water, and corn syrup together in a large, heavy-bottomed saucepan over medium-high heat. Cook, swirling pan occasionally, until sugar turns dark amber and just begins to smoke, 6 to 8 minutes. Immediately add cream and salt, stepping away from pan until bubbling and sputtering subside. Reduce heat to medium and stir just until mixture is smooth. Remove from heat.

Melt butter in a medium saucepan over medium heat. Add cocoa powder and brown sugar and whisk together until a paste forms. Slowly add milk, whisking constantly. Whisk in caramel. Bring to a simmer over medium-high heat and then reduce heat to medium-low. Stir in chocolate chips and cook, stirring, until chocolate is completely melted. Remove from heat and stir in vanilla. Pour into warm heatproof cups or mugs and spike with 1½ ounces amaretto per serving, if desired. Sprinkle with salt and serve.

Cooking Tip
You will need a large saucepan for this recipe; the addition of cream to the caramel causes the mixture to bubble aggressively.

Rosy Cheek

SERVES 4

This variation on **Winter White Chocolate** (page 55) takes a cue from Latin American **Rompope** (page 48), an eggnog-style drink made with ground almonds. Here, macadamia nuts add texture and a salty, buttery touch to the drink. But the real twist comes from pink peppercorns, whose rose flavor and mild heat add a surprising and piquant pop.

¼ cup roasted and salted macadamia nuts

3 tablespoons granulated sugar

4 cups whole milk

1 tablespoon whole pink peppercorns, crushed, plus more for garnish

6 ounces white chocolate, finely chopped

Pinch salt

2 teaspoons fresh lemon juice

6 ounces white rum, optional

Pulse nuts and sugar in a food processor until finely ground. Bring milk and peppercorns to a simmer in a medium saucepan over medium heat, stirring occasionally. Remove from heat and let steep for 15 minutes.

Strain mixture through a fine-mesh sieve into a bowl and discard solids. Return milk to saucepan and stir in nut mixture. Bring to a simmer over medium-high heat and then reduce heat to medium-low. Stir in white chocolate and salt and cook, stirring, until chocolate is completely melted. Remove from heat and stir in lemon juice. Serve in warmed cups and spike with $1\frac{1}{2}$ ounces white rum per serving, if desired.

Snowy white Mexican Wedding Cakes pair well with Rosy Cheeks and other winter cocktails. See the recipe on page 119.

White Witch

Chai, the blend of black tea and spices, can be found loose and in tea bags in most supermarkets. If you can't find the loose variety, simply cut open the bags and dump out the tea inside. Although chai tea blends contain spices, I include additional whole spices in this recipe to bolster the flavors and stand out in the rich white chocolate base.

2 teaspoons crushed green cardamom pods*

2 cinnamon sticks

1 teaspoon whole black peppercorns

½ teaspoon whole cloves

4 cups whole milk

3 tablespoons loose chai tea blend

1 (4-inch) piece fresh ginger, peeled and thinly sliced

6 ounces white chocolate, finely chopped

Pinch salt

2 teaspoons fresh lemon juice

6 ounces Bährenjäger or amaretto, optional

*To crush the pods, use the back of a chef's knife or smooth side of a meat mallet and press down. Normally, the black seeds are picked out and the shells discarded. In this recipe, however, the cardamom will be strained out, so the entire crushed pod can be added, shell and all.

Place cardamom, cinnamon, peppercorns, and cloves in a medium saucepan. Stir over medium heat until spices are fragrant, about 2 minutes. Add milk, tea, and ginger and bring to a simmer over medium heat, stirring occasionally. Remove from heat and let steep for 15 minutes.

Strain mixture through a fine-mesh sieve into a bowl and discard solids. Return milk to saucepan and bring to a simmer over medium-high heat and then reduce heat to medium-low. Stir in white chocolate and salt and cook, stirring, until chocolate is completely melted. Remove from heat and stir in lemon juice. Serve in warmed cups and spike with 1½ ounces Bährenjäger or amaretto per serving, if desired.

Cooking Tip

Lightly toasting whole spices in a dry skillet releases more of their flavor. Use this technique in both sweet and savory applications.

Persian Warmer

Green cardamom's exotic perfume is drinkable aromatherapy. Paired with one of winter's brightest fruits, it turns white hot chocolate into a veritable potion no. 9.

2 tablespoons green cardamom pods, crushed

4 cups whole milk

2 tablespoons finely grated orange zest

6 ounces white chocolate, finely chopped

Pinch salt

2 teaspoons fresh orange juice

6 ounces Grand Marnier, optional

Place cardamom in a medium saucepan. Stir over medium heat until fragrant, about 2 minutes. Add milk and orange zest and bring to a simmer over medium heat, stirring occasionally. Remove from heat and let steep for 15 minutes.

Strain mixture through a fine-mesh sieve into a bowl and discard solids. Return milk to saucepan and bring to a simmer over medium-high heat and then reduce heat to medium-low. Add white chocolate and salt and stir until chocolate is completely melted. Remove from heat and stir in orange juice. Serve in warmed cups and spike with $1\frac{1}{2}$ ounces Grand Marnier per serving, if desired.

Mama's Remedy

Milk punch is a sweetened milk drink fortified with spirits, namely bourbon and brandy. It's been around since the 1800s and is especially popular in the South. Like many other drinks in this book, it was once used medicinally. My mother's version is a better alternative to any cough syrup—just as soothing and soporific, but much easier on the way down.

4 cups whole milk

1 cup dark rum

1 ounce brandy

¼ cup honey, plus more to serve

2 cinnamon sticks

Peel of 1 orange*

Ground cinnamon, for garnish

*Remove the orange peel with a vegetable peeler, being careful to avoid the white pith, which will impart a bitter flavor.

Combine milk, rum, brandy, honey, cinnamon, and half the orange peel in a small saucepan. Bring to a simmer over medium heat, stirring, until honey is dissolved. Reduce heat to low and simmer for 5 minutes.

Meanwhile, warm cups (see page 16). Using a lighter or match, carefully run the flame along the remaining orange peel to release its oils (see page 22). Rub the flamed side of the peel along the edges of the cups. Remove and discard cinnamon sticks and orange peel and pour milk into prepared cups. Sprinkle with ground cinnamon and serve with additional honey.

Garnish Tip

Quickly and carefully running a flame along the outside of a citrus peel will release its natural oils, giving it more aroma and flavor. Rub peels along the rims of cups to add extra zing, or drop into drinks as garnishes.

Kentucky Baby

To make this variation of **Mama's Remedy**, replace the rum and brandy with **1 cup Kentucky bourbon or Bacon-Infused Bourbon (page 88)** and the honey and cinnamon sticks with **¼ cup pure maple syrup*** and **1 teaspoon pure vanilla extract.**

Pure maple syrup is delicate and prone to growing mold, yeast, and bacteria that damage its quality and flavor. Once opened, store the bottle in the refrigerator. Bring syrup to room temperature prior to serving, or warm in a small saucepan or microwave-safe bowl.

Cup of Thai

SERVES 4

Lemongrass's aromatic, citrus-like notes give this comforting milk punch a delicate yet distinctive flavor reminiscent of the tropics. Sharp ginger underscores the drink's subtleties and gives a gentle bite.

4 cups coconut milk (or 2 13.5-ounce cans)

2 stalks lemongrass, cut into thin rounds*

1 (2-inch) piece fresh ginger, peeled and sliced

Peel of 1 lime**

¼ cup coconut sugar or raw cane sugar***

6 ounces white rum

To prepare lemongrass, trim off the bottom and remove and discard the tough outer leaves. Slice the stalks crosswise with a sharp knife.

**See the orange peel tip for Mama's Remedy (page 62) for how to peel citrus.*

***Coconut sugar is a type of palm sugar derived from the coconut palm and is a common sweetener in regions where such plants are abundant, notably Southeast Asia. It is thick and sweet; I think it tastes like sugar cookie dough and often enjoy a spoonful straight out of the jar. Raw sugar is minimally processed sugarcane sugar. As opposed to its refined sibling, it is pale golden and made up of larger, coarser crystals.*

Combine milk, lemongrass, ginger, and half the lime peel in a small saucepan and bring to a simmer over medium heat. Reduce heat to low and simmer for 5 minutes. Remove from heat and let steep for 15 minutes. Strain mixture through a fine-mesh sieve into a bowl and return it to saucepan, discarding solids.

When ready to serve, warm cups (see page 16). Using a lighter or match, carefully run the flame along the remaining lime peel to release oils (see page 22). Rub the flamed edge of the peel around the rims of the cups. Return milk mixture to a simmer over medium heat. Add sugar and rum and stir until sugar is dissolved. Simmer over low heat for 2 minutes. Serve in warmed cups.

Make-Ahead Tip

The recipe can be prepared through step 1 up to 2 days in advance. Store the strained milk mixture in an airtight container in the refrigerator. When ready to serve, continue with step 2.

New Orleans Special

This twist on milk punch is a liquid version of the classic rum-flambéed bananas Foster.

4 cups whole milk

6 ounces dark rum, divided

1 ounce brandy

2 cinnamon sticks

2 bananas, peeled and sliced into
¼-inch rounds

1 tablespoon fresh lemon juice

¼ teaspoon ground cinnamon

Pinch salt

3 tablespoons unsalted butter

3 tablespoons packed dark
brown sugar

Combine milk, 4 ounces of the rum, brandy, and cinnamon in a small saucepan and bring to a simmer over medium heat. Reduce heat to low and simmer for 5 minutes.

In a small bowl, toss bananas with lemon juice, ground cinnamon, and salt. Melt butter in a medium skillet over medium-high heat. Add bananas and brown sugar and cook, stirring, until bananas are softened. Remove skillet from heat, pour in the remaining 2 ounces rum, and carefully ignite mixture with a long match. When the flame has subsided, transfer bananas and cooking liquid to saucepan with milk. Simmer until bananas are completely softened, about 10 minutes.

Strain mixture through fine-mesh sieve into a bowl and discard solids. Serve in warmed cups.

Cooking Tip

Spirits are often set aflame in dessert recipes; the alcohol burns off, leaving only flavor behind. The flames will soar briefly before dying down, so be sure to remove the skillet from the stovetop and have a clear area around you.

Nutella Melt

SERVES 4

Nutella, the addictive hazelnut-chocolate spread, melts effortlessly into milk and gets a wink and a smile from hazelnut liqueur.

4 cups whole milk

¼ cup Nutella

Pinch salt

6 ounces hazelnut liqueur, such as Frangelico

1 cup heavy cream, chilled

¼ cup confectioners' sugar

2 teaspoons instant espresso powder

¼ cup toasted hazelnuts, chopped, for garnish

Toasted coconut flakes,* for garnish

*To toast coconut flakes, arrange them in a single layer on a rimmed baking sheet and bake in a preheated 350°F oven for 7 to 10 minutes, stirring halfway through baking, until toasted. Alternatively, toast them in a large, dry skillet over medium heat, stirring occasionally, until golden, 5 to 7 minutes.

Bring milk, Nutella, and salt to a simmer in a medium saucepan over medium heat, stirring until Nutella is completely dissolved. Stir in liqueur. Turn off the heat but leave the pot on the stove while you whip the cream.

Using an electric mixer, beat cream, confectioners' sugar, and espresso powder on medium speed in a large, chilled bowl until soft peaks form, 2 to 3 minutes. (Alternatively, beat by hand using a large wire whisk.) Ladle drink into warm cups and top with whipped cream. Sprinkle with hazelnuts and coconut.

Cooking Tip

The most efficient way to remove hazelnuts' unpleasantly bitter skins is to blanch them. Bring 4 cups water and ¼ cup baking soda to boil in a large pot. Add hazelnuts and boil for 5 minutes. Drain hazelnuts in a colander and rinse them under cold running water, rubbing them against each other until most of the skins have come off. Place hazelnuts in a clean kitchen towel (one you're not too attached to, because it will stain) and rub them with the towel to remove any remaining skins.

After removing the skins, place hazelnuts on a rimmed baking sheet and bake in a preheated 350°F oven until golden brown and fragrant, about 15 minutes.

Irish Coffee

Though I don't advocate starting the workweek with a "special" brew (wink, wink), a generous splash of Irish whiskey is perfectly apropos at the end of dinner or for a weekend brunch.

1 cup heavy cream, chilled
¼ cup confectioners' sugar
½ teaspoon pure vanilla extract
6 ounces Irish whiskey
4 cups freshly brewed, strong black coffee
Granulated cane sugar, to taste
Whipped Cream for garnish

Using an electric mixer, beat cream, confectioners' sugar, and vanilla on medium speed in a large chilled bowl until soft peaks form, 2 to 3 minutes. (Alternatively, beat by hand using a large wire whisk.)

Pour 1½ ounces whiskey into each of 4 warmed cups. Add 1 cup coffee and sugar to taste and stir. Top with a dollop of whipped cream. Serve immediately.

Whipped Cream

Making whipped cream from scratch is simple and much more rewarding than squeezing it out of a can. It takes just a few minutes of quick whisking (you can always cheat and use an electric mixer) to get a jaunty dollop to stand up on the tip of your finger. For best results, always start with chilled cream and a chilled bowl, add confectioners' sugar to lightly sweeten, and you're done!

1 cup heavy cream, chilled
¼ cup confectioners' sugar

Using an electric mixer, beat cream and confectioners' sugar on medium speed in a large, chilled bowl until soft peaks form, 2 to 3 minutes. (Alternatively, beat by hand using a large wire whisk.) Makes 1½ cups.

Cafecito

Substitute **6 ounces Kahlúa or other coffee liqueur** for the whiskey.

Good Morning, Vietnam

This variation may be served chilled, like Vietnamese coffee, or hot.
Substitute **6 ounces white rum** for the whiskey, omit the sugar, and
sweeten each serving with **2 tablespoons sweetened condensed milk**.

EARL GREY MEETS FLOWER GARDEN.

The English Rose

SERVES 4

The citrusy musk of Earl Grey tea is a natural match for the floral notes of a homemade gin or vodka infusion. Pink peppercorns add a little snap to this comforting sipper. Serve it hot or iced, depending on the weather.

6 ounces **Rose-Infused Gin or Vodka** (page 105)
1 (16-ounce) pot freshly brewed Earl Grey tea*
Pink Peppercorn Simple Syrup (page 109), to taste, warmed**

For more on brewing the perfect pot of tea, see page 11.

**For an iced drink, let syrup cool to room temperature and then refrigerate until thoroughly chilled. Add just before serving.*

Pour 1¹/₂ ounces rose-infused gin or vodka in each of 4 warmed cups. Pour in tea and sweeten with pink peppercorn simple syrup to taste.

A FEW DANDY TURNS ON HIGH TEA.

The Prim and Proper
Substitute **1 pot English Breakfast tea** for the Earl Grey, **6 ounces whiskey** and **2 dashes cherry bitters** (if desired) for the alcohol, and **sugar cubes** for the simple syrup. Serve with **warm milk.**

The Stiff Upper Lip
Substitute **6 ounces Kumquat-Thyme Infused Gin or Vodka** (page 106) for the alcohol and **Lemon-Sage Simple Syrup** (page 109) for the pink peppercorn simple syrup.

Lullaby Baby
Substitute **1 pot chamomile tea** for the Earl Grey, **6 ounces Chamomile-Pear Infused Gin or Vodka** (page 106) for the alcohol, and **honey** for the simple syrup.

Chilled Winter Cocktails

Although a warm drink can melt away the frost, a strongly spirited, chilled beverage can also do the trick. Start your fête by handing out slim flutes spilling over with bubbles and spicy, ruddy, tart red beet granita. Pack friends into your living room and serve golden pineapple juice braced with Bacon-Infused Bourbon and a bonus snack of peppery candied bacon. Or have a grown-up ice cream social and serve an Affogato Speciale, an ice cream float with stout and espresso. Don't you feel cozy already?

Gather your provisions. From left to right: Margarita, a bottle of brandy, olives for the Bloody Mary garnish, Fresh Tomato Juice (page 111), citrus, salt and herbs for rimming glasses, beer, ginger ale, and more.

Brandy Alexander

The brandy Alexander is composed of cognac, crème de cacao, and a dairy product, most often half-and-half. Shaken, strained, and served chilled, the drink—believed to have been first poured in the early twentieth century—is smooth and soft. And despite being served on ice, it warms you up like a fur stole. Substitute gin for the brandy to make an original Alexander.

6 ounces cognac or brandy
4 ounces dark crème de cacao
8 ounces half-and-half
2 cups crushed ice
Freshly grated nutmeg, for garnish

Combine cognac or brandy, crème de cacao, half-and-half, and ice in a shaker. Shake vigorously and then strain into 4 chilled highball glasses. Sprinkle with nutmeg and serve.

VARIATIONS ON THE VINTAGE ORIGINAL.

Maríita's Alexander

Substitute **6 ounces dark rum** for the brandy and **¾ cup sweetened condensed milk** for the half-and-half. Combine all ingredients in a blender and blend to a slushy consistency. Pour into chilled highball glasses and serve.

Vietnamese Alexander

Iced Vietnamese coffee, with its strong dose of caffeine and creamy, rich sweetened condensed milk, will get the heart pumping and the blood flowing.

Substitute **¾ cup sweetened condensed milk** for the half-and-half, and add **¾ cup chilled espresso or very strong coffee** to the blender with the other ingredients. Blend to a slushy consistency, pour into chilled highball glasses, and serve.

Choose interesting glassware to give your parties a special look. Try vintage and discount stores for unique options that will truly stand out.

IT'S A STATE OF MIND.

Manhattan

MAKES 1

This old-school cocktail is a standard, and given that it was a favorite of Frank Sinatra and the Rat Pack, it summons visions of dark mahogany bars, slick waiters, and dapper gentlemen. It's my go-to after-hours drink, and I highly recommend that you fix one for yourself and your company to ease everyone into the evening.

2 ounces rye whiskey*

1 ounce sweet vermouth

2 dashes Angostura bitters

4 ice cubes

1 maraschino cherry

Rye is an American whiskey made by distilling a mash of grains that is at least 51 percent rye. The results are then aged in charred oak barrels. Rye is dryer and less sweet than corn-based bourbon.

Combine whiskey, vermouth, bitters, and ice in a shaker. Shake vigorously and then strain into a chilled glass. Drop in maraschino cherry and serve.

TWO DRY VERMOUTH OPTIONS.

Perfect Manhattan
Instead of 1 ounce sweet vermouth, add ½ **ounce sweet vermouth** and ½ **ounce dry vermouth.**

Dry Manhattan
To make this variation of the **Manhattan**, substitute **1 ounce dry vermouth** for the sweet vermouth.

Sweet and Lowdown
Vermouth is a fortified wine flavored with roots, herbs, and spices, among other botanicals. Sweet vermouth, as the name suggests, has a relatively high sugar content—anywhere between 10 and 15 percent—while dry vermouth clocks in at no more than 4 percent sugar.

Amore

Lemons and rosemary remind me of potted citrus trees and fragrant pines in Rome, that city of love and imagination. This granita is simple but adds vibrancy and subtle perfume to a crisp, tongue-tickling glass of prosecco. Serve it as an alternative to a plain glass of bubbly to kick off the night.

1¼ cups granulated sugar

3 tablespoons grated lemon zest

2 cups water

12 sprigs fresh rosemary, chopped, plus more for garnish

2 cups fresh lemon juice (from about 12 lemons)

Pinch salt

1 (750-milliliter) bottle prosecco, chilled

Pulse sugar and lemon zest in a food processor until sugar is damp and no strands of zest remain. (Alternatively, rub zest into sugar with fingertips.) Combine lemon sugar and water in a medium saucepan. Stir over medium-high heat until sugar is completely dissolved, about 5 minutes. Add rosemary and simmer for 10 minutes on low heat. Remove from heat and cool to room temperature.

Strain syrup through a fine-mesh sieve into a 13-by-9-inch baking pan; discard solids. Stir in lemon juice and salt. Place pan in freezer. Scrape mixture with a fork every 20 minutes until mixture is fully frozen and has a slushy consistency.

To serve, spoon 3 to 4 tablespoons granita into each of 6 champagne flutes and top with prosecco. Garnish each with a rosemary sprig.

Old-Fashioned

As sophisticated and timeless as its name suggests, the Old-Fashioned blends the brisk taste of whiskey with fruity flavors of orange and cherry to create a cocktail that's as classy as it is classic.

1 sugar cube
2 dashes Angostura bitters
2 orange slices
2½ ounces rye whiskey or bourbon
Ice cubes
3 maraschino cherries

Place sugar cube at the bottom of a lowball glass. Pour bitters directly onto sugar. Add 1 orange slice, muddle it, and then fill glass with ice cubes. Stir in whiskey or bourbon and garnish with the remaining orange slice and maraschino cherries. Serve.

THE OLD-FASHIONED, REVISITED.

New-Fangled
Cherry bitters and dark rum take this standard on a Caribbean holiday.

1 sugar cube
2 dashes cherry bitters*
Ice cubes
2½ ounces dark rum
3 maraschino cherries

Cherry bitters are available at liquor stores and online. (See page 138 for Sources.)

Place sugar cube at the bottom of a lowball glass. Pour bitters directly onto sugar. Fill glass with ice cubes, stir in rum, and garnish with maraschino cherries. Serve.

Red Red Red

MAKES 6

Ruby-skinned beets are an unexpected but welcome ingredient in cocktails: their high sugar content and bright hue make them an excellent, all-natural way to add a pop of color and flavor. Here, the beets are pureed into a granita, with spicy star anise and allspice to complement their earthy undertones, and then topped with a refreshing dose of prosecco.

8 ounces cooked beets*

1 Granny Smith apple, peeled, cored, and cut into 1-inch chunks

1 cup granulated sugar

1¼ cups water

¾ cup apple cider vinegar

6 star anise pods

2 teaspoons whole allspice berries

1 (750-milliliter) bottle prosecco, chilled

Use homemade roasted beets or store-bought vacuum-sealed beets. Avoid canned beets, which are too soft and waterlogged to use in cocktails.

Pulse beets and apples in a food processor until completely pureed. Set aside.

Combine sugar, water, vinegar, star anise, and allspice in a medium saucepan. Cook over medium-high heat, stirring, until sugar is completely dissolved, about 5 minutes. Stir in pureed beets. Remove from heat and let cool to room temperature.

Strain mixture through a fine-mesh sieve into a 13-by-9-inch baking pan; discard solids. Place pan in freezer. Scrape mixture with a fork once every 20 minutes until mixture is fully frozen and has a slushy consistency.

To serve, spoon 3 to 4 tablespoons granita into each of 6 champagne flutes. Top with prosecco.

Jaibol

MAKES 1

My grandfather, Dr. Silvio Cuadra, is ninety years old and continues to perform surgeries and make house calls in Granada, Nicaragua. He comes home for lunch and a nap, and for ages his ritual has been to sit in a rocking chair facing the atrium rose garden and have what he calls a *jaibol*. It took me years to figure out that he was saying "highball," and as a child, I was clueless about the drink's contents. It turned out to be whiskey on the rocks, but the following "jaibol" is based on my memories of the rosebushes and the sharp smell of his cologne.

1½ ounces **Rose-Infused Gin or Vodka** (page 105)

¾ ounce St-Germain elderflower liqueur

1 ounce **Blood Orange Sour Mix** (page 110)

Place gin or vodka, elderflower liqueur, and sour mix in a shaker. Shake vigorously, pour into an ice-filled highball glass, and serve.

Pear Smash

Pepper and sage give this pear-centric cocktail a savory edge, while lemon zest and ginger lend a kick and some zip. A pear-chamomile infusion rounds out the experience with an earthy, floral backdrop.

1 Bosc or Bartlett pear, peeled, cored, and grated

1 tablespoon freshly grated ginger

1 tablespoon finely grated lemon zest

2 teaspoons packed dark brown sugar

6 fresh sage leaves

Pinch freshly ground black pepper

1½ ounces **Chamomile-Pear Infused Gin or Vodka** (page 106)

1 ounce pear brandy*

2 dashes Angostura bitters

½ cup crushed ice

Pear brandy is an eau-de-vie, which in French means "water of life." It is one variety of a number of brandies distilled from fruits. Some producers tie bottles on pear tree branches, allowing the pear to grow inside the bottle. What a sight it must be!

Place pear, ginger, lemon zest, brown sugar, sage, and pepper in a shaker. Smash ingredients together with a muddler. Add gin or vodka, brandy, bitters, and ice. Shake vigorously and strain into a chilled glass. Serve.

Muddling Tip

If you don't have a muddler, use the back of a wooden spoon to smash the ingredients.

The Pear Smash is pictured to the left of What a Tart on the next page.

What a Tart

MAKES 1

In this cocktail inspired by the classic French dessert, sweet apple cider combines with bracing applejack and spicy notes of cinnamon, ginger, and mace.

2 teaspoons freshly grated ginger

1 teaspoon finely grated zest plus
   2 teaspoons juice from 1 lemon

⅛ teaspoon ground cinnamon

⅛ teaspoon ground or grated mace*

1 cup apple cider

3 ounces applejack

4 ice cubes

*Mace is the lacy exterior of the
nutmeg seed. It is sold ground,
but it may also be grated off with a
fine zester.

Place ginger, lemon zest and juice, cinnamon, and mace in a shaker. Smash ingredients together with muddler. Add apple cider and applejack and shake vigorously. Fill a glass with ice and strain drink into glass. Serve.

*The Pear Smash (left) and
What a Tart (right) cocktails
celebrate the flavors of fall.*

Golden Hog

• MAKES 4 •

Pineapple juice is fine as a cocktail mixer, but for this drink, do make your own. The fruit will break down and froth exquisitely, and nothing compares to its freshness. Bacon, in its smoky and salty glory, plays a double starring role, having infused the bourbon used in the drink as well as acting as a devilish garnish, crisp and sticky.

1 ripe pineapple, peeled, cored, and cut into 1-inch chunks

2 teaspoons pure vanilla extract

Simple Syrup (page 108) to taste

6 ounces **Bacon-Infused Bourbon,** divided

2 dashes Angostura bitters

Crushed ice

Candied bacon, for garnish (page 118)

Pulse pineapple and vanilla in a food processor until no pineapple bits remain and mixture is frothy. Add simple syrup to taste. Transfer half the mixture to a shaker and add 3 ounces of the bourbon and 1 dash of the bitters. Shake vigorously and pour into 2 ice-filled glasses. Repeat with remaining pineapple mixture, bourbon, bitters, and ice. Garnish with candied bacon and serve.

Bacon-Infused Bourbon

The process of infusing bacon into bourbon is called "fat washing," because rendered bacon fat is "washed" in bourbon for a few hours to permeate it with flavor. Try it in the Golden Hog or sneak it into Planter's Punch for a novel spin on the original rum.

1 pound bacon,* chopped

1 (750-milliliter) bottle bourbon

Use heavily smoked bacon to fully imbue the bourbon with its flavor. Mildly smoked bacon will be masked by the spirit.

Cook bacon in a large skillet over medium-high heat, stirring occasionally, until crisp. Using a slotted spoon, transfer bacon to a paper-towel-lined plate and pour fat into a large bowl. Reserve bacon for another use.

Let fat cool to room temperature, about 10 minutes, and then pour ½ cup of it into a wide-mouth 1-quart jar. Add bourbon, seal jar, and freeze for at least 6 hours. Using a spoon, scrape off and discard the fat.

Strain bourbon through a fine-mesh sieve lined with cheesecloth into a bowl. Pour bourbon through a funnel into its original bottle or store in another jar. Makes 1 (750-milliliter) bottle.

Margarita

MAKES 1

The tequila, triple sec, and lime juice libation is alchemy in a glass: witness its popularity—and notoriety—at bars everywhere. Though this drink is served chilled and commonly associated with summer, there's no denying its bracing and warming effects.

¼ cup kosher salt

½ lime

2 ounces tequila

1 ounce triple sec or Cointreau

2 tablespoons lime juice or homemade **Lime Sour Mix** (page 110)

Spread salt in a layer on a small plate or saucer. Rub the rim of a glass with lime to moisten. Dip rim into salt, shaking off excess. Fill glass with ice.

Place tequila, triple sec, and lime juice or sour mix in a shaker. Shake vigorously and strain into glass. Serve.

Más Picante

For an extra-spicy Margarita, replace regular tequila with **Serrano-Lime Infused Tequila** (page 104) or **Jalapeño-Mint-Cilantro Infused Tequila** (page 105).

Green with Envy Margarita

Place ¼ lemongrass stalk (sliced and smashed with the back of knife), ¼ teaspoon kosher salt, 1½ ounces Lime Sour Mix (page 110), 2 tablespoons cilantro leaves (chopped), and 2 tablespoons mint leaves (chopped) in a shaker with ice. Proceed with recipe. Garnish with fresh cilantro and mint.

Red Lipstick Margarita

Add 1 ounce triple sec or ginger liqueur, such as Domaine de Canton* and 2 tablespoons Blood Orange Sour Mix (page 110) in shaker with ice. Proceed with recipe. Garnish with a blood orange wedge.

Domaine de Canton is a sharp, intensely fragrant liqueur made of fresh ginger. It adds a bold note to this cocktail.

Affogato Speciale

Affogato literally translates into "drowned," an apt descriptor of this traditional Italian desert drink that consists of a scoop of gelato drowned in a shot of hot espresso. In this rendition, chocolate stout and amaretto are added to make a version of the drink that ups the ante and results in a very grown-up ice cream float—a perfect after-dinner treat.

1 scoop vanilla ice cream or gelato

2 ounces amaretto

1 (2-ounce) shot espresso

6 ounces chocolate stout

Place ice cream in a tall glass. Pour liqueur, espresso, and stout over top. Serve with a spoon.

A CREAMSICLE-INSPIRED VARIATION.

Peachy Keen Affogato

Substitute **bourbon** for the almond liqueur and **peach lambic*** for the chocolate stout. Garnish with a flamed orange rind (see page 22 for instructions).

*Lambic is a Belgian beer flavored with fruits. It comes in a variety of flavors, including raspberry, black currant, grape, and strawberry. If you make affogato with any of these flavors (rather than peach), substitute vodka, gin, crème de cassis, or Chambord for the bourbon.

Bloody Mary

MAKES 1

A staple on brunch menus, the bloody Mary is the cure-all for a booze-soaked evening. For even better flavor (and healthfulness), use fresh tomato juice rather than canned, which is dense with sodium and not very refreshing.

½ cup **Fresh Tomato Juice** (page 111)

2 ounces vodka or **Celery–Black Pepper Infused Vodka** (page 105)

2 small celery stalks with leaves

1 lemon wedge

2 pimento-stuffed olives

2 cocktail onions

Place tomato juice and vodka in a shaker. Shake vigorously and pour into an ice-filled glass. Garnish with celery, lemon, olives, and onions.

A Round for the House

This recipe can be easily multiplied to make a pitcher. The Fresh Tomato Juice recipe yields 2 cups, so plan ahead and make enough to serve a crowd.

Bloody María

Substitute **Jalapeño-Mint-Cilantro Infused Tequila** (page 105) for the vodka and garnish with **cilantro sprigs and pickled jalapeños.**

Shandy

The shandy, or shandygaff, sounds like a J. R. R. Tolkien invention, but in fact it is a real drink made by combining beer with a carbonated beverage. I prefer it with a strong ginger beer, whose assertive flavor plays well with lagers.

6 ounces lager

4 ounces ginger beer*

Available in both nonalcoholic and alcoholic varieties, ginger beer tastes a bit like ginger ale but with a kickier ginger flavor.

Pour lager into a chilled glass. Add ginger beer and serve.

MORE DANDY SHANDIES.

Melba Shandy

Substitute **peach lambic** for the lager and add **2 ounces raspberry liqueur**, such as Chambord.

Greyhound Shandy

Omit the ginger beer and combine **2 ounces fresh grapefruit juice**, **2 ounces club soda**, and add **2 ounces vodka** with the lager.

Black Russian

The black russian is a sleek, classic cocktail made of vodka (that's where the *Russian* comes in) and coffee liqueur (you guessed it: color reference).

2 ounces vodka

1 ounce coffee liqueur, such as Kahlúa

Fill a rocks glass with ice. Pour in vodka and coffee liqueur over ice and stir. Serve.

NOW WITH A SPLASH OF CREAM.

White Russian

Add **1 ounce heavy cream** and serve immediately.

Mixing Tip

Make these drinks a boozy weekend brunch item and add an extra kick of caffeine by serving them over coffee ice cubes: brew a pot of coffee, let cool to room temperature, pour into ice trays, and freeze until firm.

The White Russian, mixed with a splash of heavy cream, is to the left, with its darker dairy-free Black Russian counterpart to the right.

Underpinnings: Infused Liquors, Simple Syrups, Etc.

Infused liquors lay the foundation for many cocktails. Like a silk slip under a form-fitting dress, the flavored spirit adds a subtle layer that will make the final product a knockout. In a similar manner, simple syrups made with spice and herb blends take a plain drink to new levels. Try these in specific recipes throughout the book, or bottle and label them to give to friends. Another idea: bring ingredients to a party to make a specialty cocktail.

All year long you can use fresh produce to flavor spirits. Try fruits, vegetables, herbs, edible flowers, and peppers—whatever's in season.

Infused Liquors

When included in a cocktail, spirits are combined with other flavoring ingredients, but they themselves can be infused. The infusion process is simple, and you can experiment with any number of ingredients. Start with these recipes and then test out your own combinations. If you're unsure about your ingredients, start with a small batch.

Follow the first step in each of the following recipes, then proceed with these additional steps: Taste infusion every day; it is ready when the flavor intensity you desire has been reached. Strain infusion through a fine-mesh sieve into a clean vessel; discard solids. Use a funnel to return infusion to its original jar. Infused liquor will keep indefinitely.

FRAGRANT AND FLAVORFUL VARIATIONS.

Serrano-Lime Infused Tequila

Tequila is fragrant and distinctive, but it welcomes a layer of heat and zest. Try this infusion in a **Margarita** (page 90) and **Bloody María** (page 95).

4 fresh serrano chiles,* scrubbed and halved lengthwise

2 limes, scrubbed and quartered

1 (750-milliliter) bottle white or silver tequila

Serranos are bright green, slender, tapered peppers approximately 2 inches long. They are commonly found in the produce section of supermarkets. Their heat comes from the ribs and seeds—these can be removed and discarded, if desired.

Place chiles and limes in a 1-quart airtight glass jar or other lidded container. Pour in tequila, close tightly, and shake. Store in a cool, dark place for 3 to 5 days, shaking jar 2 to 3 times a day to redistribute ingredients.

Jalapeño-Mint-Cilantro Infused Tequila

Substitute **4 fresh jalapeños** for the serranos and **1 cup each fresh cilantro sprigs and mint leaves** for the limes.

Cooking Tip

Serrano chiles are extremely hot. You can lessen the burn but keep some of the kick by making a quick infusion. Infuse the tequila with lime for 3 days and then add the chiles. Infuse for as little as 1 hour and up to 1 day, testing throughout the infusion process until the desired heat level and flavor are achieved.

Celery–Black Pepper Infused Vodka

Vodka, like gin, is one of the easiest spirits to infuse, for it provides a clean canvas. This version is well-suited for use in the **Bloody Mary** (page 94) in particular.

2 tablespoons whole black peppercorns
4 celery stalks, scrubbed and trimmed to fit infusing vessel
1 (750-milliliter) bottle vodka

Place peppercorns in a small skillet and stir over medium heat until fragrant, about 2 minutes. Combine peppercorns and celery in a 1-quart airtight glass jar or other lidded container. Pour in vodka, close tightly, and shake. Store in a cool, dark place for 3 to 5 days, shaking jar 2 to 3 times a day to redistribute ingredients.

Rose-Infused Gin or Vodka

Dried roses aren't just for filling sachets; saturated in gin or vodka, they perfume cocktails and turn them into elixirs. As a variation, try adding 2 tablespoons whole black peppercorns to this infusion.

¼ cup edible dried rosebuds*
1 (750-milliliter) bottle gin or vodka

Edible dried rosebuds are available at specialty stores and online. See page 138 for Sources.

Place rosebuds in a 1-quart airtight glass jar or other lidded container. Pour in gin or vodka, close tightly, and shake. Store in a cool, dark place for 3 to 5 days, shaking jar 2 to 3 times a day to redistribute ingredients.

(continued)

(continued from previous page)

Blackberry-Thyme Infused Gin or Vodka

Tart blackberries complement lemony, herbal thyme for an infusion that can be stirred or shaken into cocktails. It can even be enjoyed on the rocks—just add twist of lemon rind.

1 pint blackberries
1 bunch thyme
1 (750-milliliter) bottle gin or vodka

Place blackberries and thyme in a 1-quart airtight glass jar or other lidded container. Pour in gin or vodka, close tightly, and shake. Store in a cool, dark place for 3 to 5 days, shaking jar 2 to 3 times a day to redistribute ingredients.

Kumquat-Thyme Infused Gin
Substitute **1½ cups kumquats**, sliced, for the blackberries.

Chamomile-Pear Infused Gin or Vodka

Chamomile flowers taste of mellow afternoon sunshine. In this infusion, their wildflower essence blends effortlessly with pears.

1 cup dried chamomile flowers*
2 pears, peeled and diced
1 (750-milliliter) bottle gin or vodka

Edible dried chamomile flowers are available at specialty stores and online. See page 138 for Sources.

Place flowers and pears in a 1-quart airtight glass jar or other lidded container. Pour in gin or vodka, close tightly, and shake. Store in a cool, dark place for 3 to 5 days, shaking jar 2 to 3 times a day to redistribute ingredients.

Pineapple-Spice Infused Rum

Rum, spices, and pineapple are often mixed together in cocktails, especially those with a Caribbean inflection. This homemade spiced rum is made with fresh pineapple, so it gives cocktails a jump start on those flavors. Keep some on hand year-round for warm-weather drinks.

1 tablespoon whole allspice berries
2 teaspoons whole cloves
1 teaspoon whole black peppercorns
3 cinnamon sticks
1 pineapple, peeled and cubed
1 (750-milliliter) bottle dark rum

Place allspice, cloves, peppercorns, and cinnamon in a small skillet and stir over medium heat until fragrant, about 2 minutes. Place spices and pineapples in a 1-quart airtight glass jar or other lidded container. Pour in rum, close tightly, and shake. Store in a cool, dark place for 3 to 5 days, shaking jar 2 to 3 times a day to redistribute ingredients.

Simple Syrup

Simple syrup is, as the name states, simple. Keep this formula in your back pocket—ratios for simple syrups vary according to the desired thickness of the final product, but I prefer this one-to-one ratio for a pourable and easy-to-dissolve consistency.

1 cup granulated sugar
1 cup water

Combine sugar and water in a small saucepan. Bring to a simmer over medium heat and cook, stirring, until sugar is completely dissolved. Let cool to room temperature and store, refrigerated, in an airtight container. Syrup will keep indefinitely.

VARIATIONS ON A SIMPLE THEME.

Honey Syrup

Honey dissolves perfectly in hot beverages, but add it to a chilled liquid and it will sink to the bottom and impart no sweetness. Honey syrup, on the other hand, is diluted and blends easily into even the iciest of drinks.

1 cup honey
1 cup water

Combine honey and water in a small saucepan. Bring to a simmer over medium heat and cook, stirring, until honey is completely dissolved. Let cool to room temperature and store, refrigerated, in an airtight container. Syrup will keep indefinitely. *Makes 2 cups.*

A Key Ingredient

This most basic of sweeteners blends easily into chilled drinks, whereas a solid like granulated sugar would simply sit undissolved at the bottom of the glass. Keep it on hand to sweeten any drinks you think need a hit of sugar, including iced tea and lemonade.

Lemon-Sage Simple Syrup

Bright lemon and peppery sage are perfect teammates and make this syrup sing.

1½ cups granulated sugar
½ cup fresh sage leaves
2 tablespoons finely grated zest plus ½ cup lemon juice (from about 4 lemons)
½ cup water
Pinch salt

Pulse sugar, sage, and lemon zest in a food processor until sugar is damp and no zest strands remain. Combine sugar mixture, lemon juice, water, and salt in a medium saucepan. Cook over medium-high heat, stirring, until sugar is completely dissolved, about 5 minutes. Remove from heat and let cool to room temperature. Strain through a ne-mesh sieve and discard solids. Refrigerate syrup for up to 1 month in an airtight container.

Pink Peppercorn Simple Syrup

Give simple syrup a kick with a dash of crushed pink peppercorn.

1½ cups granulated sugar
1 cup water
¼ cup pink peppercorns, crushed

Combine sugar, water, and pink peppercorns in a medium saucepan. Cook over medium-high heat, stirring, until sugar is completely dissolved, about 5 minutes. Remove from heat and let cool to room temperature. Strain through a fine-mesh sieve and discard solids. Refrigerate for up to 1 month in an airtight container.

Homemade Sour Mix

MAKES 3 CUPS

Mass-produced sour mix, or bar mix, is sold by the gallon and, though convenient, the neon-green concoction is cloying and lacks the sour punch that fresh citrus delivers. Making it at home is no great feat: a quick boil of sugar and water, a squeeze of lemon and lime, and you're done. Your cocktails will be transformed.

Use this recipe in a **Margarita** (page 90) or to flavor any simple cocktail, like vodka on the rocks.

1 cup granulated sugar
2 tablespoons finely grated lemon zest
2 tablespoons finely grated lime zest
1 cup water
1 cup fresh lemon juice (from about 6 lemons), strained
1 cup fresh lime juice (from about 10 limes), strained

Pulse sugar and zests in a food processor until sugar is damp and no zest strands remain. (Alternatively, rub zest into sugar with fingertips.) Combine sugar and water in a small saucepan and cook over medium heat, stirring, until sugar is completely dissolved. Let syrup cool to room temperature and then stir in lemon and lime juices. Refrigerate for up to 1 month in an airtight container.

TWO PUCKER-WORTHY OPTIONS.

Lime Sour Mix
Use **1 ½ cups fresh lime juice** and **½ cup fresh lemon juice.**

Blood Orange Sour Mix
Use **3 tablespoons finely grated blood orange zest, 2 cups fresh blood orange juice,* and 2 tablespoons fresh lemon juice.**

*Blood oranges, like other citrus fruits, are available in the winter, typically from December through March. Varieties include the intensely hued Moro and Tarocco. The flesh of these oranges is stunningly saturated with shades ranging from dark pink to maroon. Their flavor is tart and sweet, with notes of red berry.

Fresh Tomato Juice

Canned tomato juice is often high in sodium, which doesn't make for refreshing sipping. And when making your own is so simple, there's no reason not to. For this recipe, smaller varieties of tomatoes work well and are a better option in winter months, when supermarket tomatoes lack flavor.

2 pounds cherry or grape tomatoes, chopped

2 celery ribs, chopped

2 medium carrots, peeled and grated

½ cup flat-leaf parsley, chopped

¼ cup cilantro leaves, chopped (optional)

2 tablespoons granulated sugar

2 tablespoons fresh lemon juice, plus more to taste

2 teaspoons olive brine, plus more to taste

1 tablespoon Worcestershire sauce

1 tablespoon finely grated fresh horseradish

1½ teaspoons salt, plus more to taste

Freshly ground black pepper to taste

Celery salt, to taste (optional)

Hot sauce, to taste

Pulse all ingredients together in a food processor and then strain through a fine-mesh sieve. Season to taste with additional salt, celery salt, pepper, hot sauce, olive brine, and/or lemon juice. Stir before serving to incorporate any solids that have settled at the bottom.

Small Bites

I'm a hostess who likes to feed her guests, even when they protest about just having eaten dinner. To that end, these bites are tempting to even the most contrary of people. You'll find recipes for a few posh treats, like roasted marrow bones and bagna cauda, as well as casual treats like party mix and freshly fried (and *too* easy) doughnuts.

A tasty spread (from left to right): Cheese and Charcuterie Board, Mexican Wedding Cakes, Cheater Doughnuts, and Hot Toddies, all nestled among nuts and citrus garnishes.

Homemade Marshmallows

MAKES ABOUT 35 (2-INCH) MARSHMALLOWS

Once you've tasted a homemade marshmallow, you'll never go slumming with the store-bought styrofoam ones again. The trick to successful mallows is to heat syrup to the proper temperature, which is easily done with a candy thermometer and some patience.

Nonstick cooking spray
Confectioners' sugar, for dusting
1 cup cold water, divided
3 (¼-ounce) envelopes unflavored gelatin
2 cups granulated sugar
⅔ cup light corn syrup
¼ teaspoon salt
2 teaspoons pure vanilla extract

Want More Fluff?
For thicker marshmallows, replace the 13-by-9-inch pan with an 8-by-8-inch pan. This variation makes about 16 (2-inch) marshmallows.

Line a 13-by-9-inch baking pan with foil, allowing about 2 inches of excess to hang over opposite ends. Turn the pan 90 degrees and line with a second sheet of foil, again allowing 2 inches of excess to hang over the other ends. You should have a cross-shaped lining. Coat foil lightly with nonstick spray and sprinkle generously with confectioners' sugar.

Pour ½ cup of the cold water into a large bowl or the bowl of a heavy-duty electric mixer fitted with the whisk attachment. Sprinkle gelatin over water. Let stand until gelatin softens and absorbs water, 10 to 15 minutes.

Meanwhile, combine sugar, corn syrup, salt, and the remaining ½ cup cold water in a medium heavy-bottomed saucepan. Cook, stirring, over medium heat, until sugar and syrup are completely dissolved, brushing down sides of pan with a wet pastry brush to prevent sugar granules from scorching the sides of the pan. Attach a candy thermometer to side of pan, increase heat to medium-high, and bring mixture to boil. Boil, without stirring, until syrup reaches 240°F, about 8 minutes. Immediately remove from heat.

With mixer on low speed, slowly pour hot syrup into gelatin in a slow, steady stream. Gradually increase mixer speed to high and beat until mixture is very thick and stiff and mixing bowl is cool to the touch, about 15 minutes. Add vanilla and continue beating just until blended, about 30 seconds.

Spray a rubber spatula with cooking spray and use it to scrape marshmallow mixture into prepared pan. Smooth top with spatula and dust with confectioners' sugar. Let mixture stand uncovered at room temperature until firm, about 4 hours.

Sift a generous amount of confectioners' sugar onto a clean, dry cutting board. Turn out marshmallow slab onto board and peel off and discard foil. Sift more confectioners' sugar over marshmallow slab. Coat a large sharp knife with nonstick spray and use it to cut marshmallows into squares. Fill a large bowl with confectioners' sugar and toss marshmallows to coat. Store in airtight container at room temperature for up to 1 week.

AND EVERYTHING NICE

Peppermint Marshmallows
Add **2 teaspoons peppermint extract** along with the vanilla extract.

Orange Blossom Marshmallows
Add **2 teaspoons orange extract** along with the vanilla extract.

Lavender Marshmallows
Add **1 teaspoon lavender extract** along with the vanilla extract.

Rose Marshmallows
Add **2 teaspoons rose water** along with the vanilla extract.

Candied Bacon

MAKES 16 STRIPS

Smoky, crunchy, fatty bacon strips are good on their own, but a spiced shellac makes them even better. Arrange these porky snacks in a cup, and definitely use them to garnish the **Golden Hog** (page 88).

16 strips thick-cut bacon

¼ cup packed dark brown sugar

1 teaspoon ground cinnamon

1 teaspoon ground ginger

½ teaspoon freshly ground black pepper

¼ teaspoon ground cumin

¼ teaspoon Aleppo pepper*

Aleppo is type of crushed red pepper native to Syria. Available at specialty markets (see page 138 for Sources), it is piquant and vibrant.

Adjust 2 oven racks to upper-middle and lower-middle positions and preheat oven to 400°F. Line 2 rimmed baking sheets with foil. Arrange 8 strips of bacon on each prepared baking sheet.

In small bowl, stir together brown sugar, cinnamon, ginger, black pepper, cumin, and Aleppo pepper. Rub sugar mixture over both sides of bacon. Once coated, rearrange strips in a single layer.

Bake, turning once halfway through cooking, until bacon is crisp and golden, 16 to 18 minutes. Transfer sheet to cooling rack and cool bacon to room temperature.

Make-Ahead Tip

Prepare the bacon up to 1 day in advance and store, refrigerated, in a single layer in an airtight container. Before serving, warm on a baking sheet in a preheated 350°F oven for about 5 minutes, or until crisp.

Orange, Cardamom, and Pistachio Mexican Wedding Cakes

MAKES ABOUT 32 COOKIES

Mexican Wedding Cakes aren't really cakes at all; they're rich, crumbly shortbread cookies made with butter and confectioners' sugar. Certain versions are made with lard, which adds an unmistakable savory, porky flavor (if you have access to pure lard, try it here). This recipe and its variations make use of different blends of spices, nuts, and raisins.

1 cup roasted and salted shelled pistachios

1 tablespoon finely grated orange zest

1 cup (2 sticks) unsalted butter, at room temperature

2 cups confectioners' sugar, divided

2 teaspoons pure vanilla extract

2 cups all-purpose flour

¾ teaspoon plus ⅛ teaspoon ground cardamom, divided

¼ teaspoon salt

⅛ teaspoon ground cinnamon

Pulse pistachios and orange zest in a food processor until pistachios are coarsely ground. Set aside.

Using an electric mixer, beat butter on medium-high speed in a large bowl until light and fluffy, about 1 minute. Stop mixer and add ½ cup of the confectioners' sugar. Beat on low speed until fully incorporated, about 30 seconds. Scrape sides and bottom of bowl with a rubber spatula; add vanilla. Mix on medium-high speed until incorporated, about 10 seconds.

Stop mixer and add flour, ¾ teaspoon of the cardamom, salt, and nut mixture; mix on medium-low speed until dough comes together, 60 to 90 seconds. With rubber spatula, scrape sides and bottom of bowl and pat dough down to bring it together. Cover bowl with plastic wrap and refrigerate for 30 minutes.

Meanwhile, adjust an oven rack to the middle position and preheat oven to 350°F. Line 2 baking sheets with parchment paper.

Scoop a tablespoonful of dough onto prepared baking sheets and then quickly roll pieces between palms into balls and place them ½ inch apart on prepared sheets. Lightly press dough to a thickness of ½ inch.

Bake until cookies are golden brown on bottom (they will remain pale on top), 15 to 20 minutes.

(continued)

(continued from previous page)

While cookies bake, whisk together the remaining 1½ cups confectioners' sugar, the remaining ⅛ teaspoon cardamom, and cinnamon in large bowl; set aside.

Transfer baking sheet to cooling rack and cool cookies on sheet for 5 minutes. Gently toss warm cookies in sugar mixture and transfer to cooling rack to cool completely, 30 to 60 minutes.

Cookies will keep for up to 1 week stored in an airtight container.

MORE NUTTY OPTIONS TO TRY.

Pecan Mexican Wedding Cakes

Substitute **1 cup toasted and chopped pecans** for the pistachios and omit the cardamom.

Boozy Walnut-Raisin Wedding Cakes

Combine ¼ **cup brandy** and ½ **cup golden raisins** in a small heatproof bowl and microwave for 1 to 2 minutes, until raisins are plump and most of the liquid is absorbed; let cool to room temperature and discard any excess liquid. Substitute **1 cup toasted and chopped walnuts** for the pistachios, omit the cardamom, and stir in the cooled raisins along with the nuts.

Grilled Pimento Cheese Sandwiches

MAKES 16 HALF SANDWICHES

Sandwiches made with buttery, toasted bread and oozing with cheese are arguably one of the best foods in the world. This recipe and the variations that follow are a bit more sophisticated than the kids' menu staple—and easier to eat while juggling a cocktail.

¼ cup mayonnaise, divided

1 tablespoon finely grated yellow onion

1 teaspoon dry mustard

⅛ teaspoon cayenne pepper

2 cups (8 ounces) finely grated extra-sharp cheddar cheese

4 ounces cream cheese, softened

½ cup drained jarred pimentos, finely chopped

1 tablespoon Worcestershire sauce

Salt and pepper, to taste

16 slices sturdy white sandwich bread, crusts trimmed

6 tablespoons (¾ stick) unsalted butter, melted

Adjust oven racks to the upper-middle and lower-middle positions and preheat oven to 450°F. Place 1 rimmed baking sheet on each rack.

Melt 2 tablespoons of the mayonnaise in a small skillet over medium heat. Add onion, dry mustard, and cayenne and cook, stirring often, until onion is softened, about 3 minutes. Transfer to a large bowl and add cheddar cheese, cream cheese, pimentos, Worcestershire, and the remaining 2 tablespoons mayonnaise. Stir to thoroughly combine and season to taste with salt and pepper.

Spread about ¼ cup pimento cheese on 8 slices of bread and press the remaining 8 slices over them. Brush both sides of each sandwich with melted butter. Transfer heated baking sheets to cooling racks. Arrange 8 sandwiches on one sheet and return to middle rack of oven. Carefully press second baking sheet on top. Bake until sandwiches are golden, 6 to 8 minutes.

Transfer sandwiches to cooling rack and let rest for 2 minutes before cutting in half.

SWANKY TAKES ON THE BASIC.

Grilled Blue Cheese and Watercress Sandwiches

Substitute 6 ounces crumbled blue cheese, such as Roquefort or Stilton, for the cheddar and ½ cup watercress, chopped, for the pimentos. These sandwiches go splendidly with the **Red Red Red** cocktail (page 82).

Grilled Parmesan, Sage, and Honey Sandwiches

Cook ½ **cup sage leaves** in 1 tablespoon unsalted butter in a small skillet over medium heat until crisp, 3 to 5 minutes. Transfer to a paper towel and pat dry. Crumble and add to bowl with cheddar and cream cheese. Stir in **1 cup (2 ounces) finely grated Parmesan cheese.** Substitute **1 teaspoon Aleppo pepper** for the cayenne and add **2 tablespoons honey.** Omit the pimentos and Worcestershire and mix the mayonnaise-honey mixture into the cheese.

Party Mix

Everyone is familiar with the cereal-based party mix, full of different crunchy bits and hits of salt and garlic powder. Most times these mixes are an afterthought, especially when they are premixed and served straight out of a bag. These homemade editions—one salty, one sweet—are truly addictive, bursting with deep, smoky, buttery, caramel flavor. Serve them with chilled cocktails and punches, or wrap them up and give them away.

8 cups Chex cereal (wheat, corn, rice, or a combination)

2 cups roasted and salted marcona almonds*

2 cups bite-sized pretzels

3 cups plain pita chips or bagel chips, broken into 1-inch pieces

¾ cup (1½ sticks) unsalted butter

3 garlic cloves, minced

1 tablespoon smoked paprika**

1 tablespoon mustard powder (such as Coleman's)

1 teaspoon salt

½ teaspoon pepper

2 tablespoons Worcestershire sauce

3 tablespoons black mustard seeds

*Marcona almonds hail from Spain and are a bit rounder than the usual pointed fingernail-shaped ones we see most often. They are also sweeter and meatier and add a distinctive touch to recipes. Serve them on their own or alongside cured olives, cheeses, and charcuterie.

**Smoked paprika is different from hot or sweet types. It is sold as "smoked."

Adjust oven racks to the upper-middle and lower-middle positions and preheat oven to 250°F. In a large bowl, toss to combine cereal, almonds, pretzels, and pita chips.

Melt butter in a small saucepan over medium heat. Stir in garlic, smoked paprika, mustard powder, salt, and pepper and cook, stirring, until mixture is fragrant, about 1 minute. Stir in Worcestershire sauce and black mustard seeds.

Pour spice mixture over cereal mixture and toss with a rubber spatula until evenly coated. Divide mixture between 2 rimmed baking sheets, spreading into an even layer. Bake, stirring every 15 minutes, until dry and toasted, 45 to 60 minutes.

Transfer sheets to cooling racks and let cool completely. Party Mix may be made up to 1 week in advance and stored in an airtight container.

A SUBTLY SWEET EDITION.

Brown Butter–Pecan Party Mix

Substitute **3 cups pecans, very coarsely chopped**, for the marcona almonds. Omit the garlic, smoked paprika, mustard powder, pepper, Worcestershire, and mustard seeds. Cook butter until the solids turn brown and sink to the bottom, about 6 to 8 minutes, and then stir in ¼ **cup packed dark brown sugar**, **1 tablespoon ground ginger**, **2 teaspoons ground cinnamon**, **1 teaspoon salt**, and ¼ **cup bourbon**. Proceed with recipe as above.

Bagna Cauda

Bagna cauda (pronounced BAH-nyah COW-dah) means "hot bath" in Italian. The pungent dip, served warm, is made of butter, garlic, oil, and anchovies and is traditionally served with crudités, whose cool crispness balances the brine and garlic. But I like to add a loaf of crusty bread as well.

½ cup (1 stick) unsalted butter

10 garlic cloves, thinly sliced

24 oil-packed anchovies, finely chopped

½ cup extra-virgin olive oil

Freshly ground black pepper, to taste

Crunchy vegetables like fennel, radicchio, or endive, for serving

Crusty bread, for serving

Melt butter in a medium saucepan over low heat. Add garlic and cook, stirring, until softened and fragrant, 2 to 3 minutes. Stir in anchovies and continue to stir while drizzling in olive oil. Reduce heat to low and simmer about 10 minutes. Season with pepper. Serve warm with vegetables.

Cheater Doughnuts

MAKES 8 LARGE OR 10 SMALL DOUGHNUTS AND DOUGHNUT HOLES

Store-bought biscuit dough makes easy work of these irresistible fried confections, which lend themselves to a dusting or glaze of your favorite flavors, whether savory or sweet. Toss them in simple cinnamon sugar, dip them in warm maple syrup (give your guests a small bowl), or add some extra zing with a spiced sugar coating, citrus, or vanilla bean sugar. Serve them with **Eve's Addiction** and its variations (pages 36 and 37).

1 can store-bought biscuit dough,*
   such as Pillsbury
8 cups vegetable oil
Glaze or coating of your choice, for
   decorating (see recipes, below)

Pillsbury biscuits work well for this recipe. One roll of the Buttermilk variety yields 10 small (about 2½ inches in diameter) doughnuts and 10 doughnut holes; use a ½-inch round cutter to punch out the holes. One roll of the Grands Homestyle Buttermilk variety yields 8 large (about 3½ inches in diameter) doughnuts and 8 doughnut holes; use a 1-inch round cutter to punch out the holes.

Prep Tip
Make the glazes while the oil for the doughnuts is heating, then stir to recombine right before pouring over the doughnuts.

Cut out centers of biscuits with a small circle cutter to make doughnut holes.

Fill a Dutch oven or large skillet with high sides with oil to a depth of 1 to 1½ inches and heat over medium-high heat until temperature registers 350°F. Add half of the doughnuts and half of the doughnut holes and fry until the bottoms turn golden brown, 1 to 1½ minutes for small doughnuts and 2 to 2½ minutes for large doughnuts. Using chopsticks or the handles of 2 wooden spoons, flip doughnuts and holes and fry until golden brown all over, 1 to 2 minutes longer.

Transfer doughnuts to a paper-towel-lined plate and let cool slightly, 1 to 2 minutes, before dipping in glaze or coating in sugar (see recipes, below). Serve warm.

Plain Jane Glaze
2 cups confectioners' sugar
¼ teaspoon salt
8 tablespoons (1 stick) unsalted butter, melted
¼ cup whole milk
1 teaspoon pure vanilla extract

Place confectioners' sugar and salt in a medium bowl. Whisk in melted butter, milk, and vanilla until smooth.

Chocolate Glaze

1 cup confectioners' sugar

1 cup unsweetened cocoa powder

¼ teaspoon salt

¾ cup whole milk

Place confectioners' sugar, cocoa powder, and salt in medium bowl. Whisk in milk until smooth.

Brown Butter Glaze

8 tablespoons (1 stick) unsalted butter, cut into 8 pieces

2 cups confectioners' sugar

¼ teaspoon salt

1 teaspoon pure vanilla extract

¼ cup whole milk

Melt butter in a small stainless-steel saucepan over medium-high heat and cook for 5 to 8 minutes, swirling the pan occasionally. You will know it is almost done when the foam begins to subside. Once the solids are caramel brown, remove pan from heat and immediately pour butter into a medium bowl, scraping in all the solids from the pan. Add confectioners' sugar, salt, and vanilla extract and whisk until smooth.

Spicy Sage Sugar

3 tablespoons unsalted butter

¾ cup sage leaves

1 cup granulated sugar

½ teaspoon kosher salt

½ teaspoon Aleppo pepper or red pepper flakes

Melt butter in a small skillet over medium heat. Add sage leaves and cook, stirring occasionally, until crisp, 2 to 3 minutes. Transfer to a paper-towel-lined plate.

Crumble sage with fingertips and combine with sugar, salt, and Aleppo pepper in a large shallow dish.

Cheese and Charcuterie Board

This recipe is more a guide to assembling a board. You can combine any amount and variety of cured and smoked meats and cheeses—whatever suits your tastes. Just be sure to have a good balance of flavors and textures.

Add crackers, good bread, roasted and salted nuts, fruit spreads, and dried fruits to fill out the plate and allow guests to build their own snacks.

The flavor of meats and cheeses peaks at room temperature. For the optimal experience, arrange your platter, cover loosely with plastic wrap, and let sit for at least an hour prior to serving.

Arrange cheeses on a sheet of parchment paper and write the type of cheese and its flavor profile on the parchment, so guests know what they're eating.

How Much Per Person?

I usually provide ⅛ pound per person for meats, rounding up slightly because I like a full board. For cheeses, I serve about ¼ pound of each variety but often buy more, depending on the size of the wedge.

Pigs on Cushions

Pigs in blankets are the first thing to fly off the table at parties. For this version, I opt for homemade buttermilk biscuits instead of the usual crescent roll wrapper. These will be popular—be ready to make a bunch of batches.

For the Sausages

3 tablespoons guava or grape jelly*

3 tablespoons ketchup

2 teaspoons spicy mustard, plus more for serving

2 teaspoons apple cider vinegar

¼ teaspoon freshly ground black pepper

Pinch cayenne pepper

1 tablespoon unsalted butter

16 cocktail sausages, such as Hillshire Farm Lit'l Smokies

*Guava jelly adds a tart and unique flavor to the glaze; look for it in the Latin-American aisle at the supermarket. If you can't find it, use grape jelly instead.

For the Sausages: In a small bowl, whisk together jelly, ketchup, mustard, vinegar, black pepper, and cayenne. Melt butter in a medium skillet over medium-high heat. Add sausages and cook, stirring occasionally, until browned, about 3 minutes. Add jelly mixture to skillet and cook, stirring occasionally, until mixture is thick and syrupy, 3 to 4 minutes. Remove from heat.

For the Biscuits: Adjust an oven rack to the middle position and preheat oven to 425°F. Line a rimmed baking sheet with parchment paper and lightly coat with baking spray.

Combine flour, cake flour, baking powder, sugar, salt, and baking soda in a large bowl. Add chilled butter and, using two knives, cut into dry ingredients until mixture resembles a coarse meal. Add ¾ cup buttermilk and stir with a wooden spoon just until combined. If mixture looks dry, add more buttermilk, 1 tablespoon at a time, until dough is cohesive.

For the Biscuits

Baking spray*

1 cup all-purpose flour, plus more
   for dusting counter

½ cup cake flour**

1½ teaspoons baking powder

2 teaspoons sugar

¾ teaspoons salt

¼ teaspoon baking soda

4 tablespoons unsalted butter cut
   into ¼-inch pieces, chilled

¾ cup buttermilk, chilled, plus more
   if needed

*Cooking spray will grease your pans,
but baking spray will mimic the results
of greasing and flouring with less
effort.

**The addition of cake flour, which
contains less protein than all-purpose,
to the batter makes biscuits impossibly
light and fluffy.

Turn dough out onto a lightly floured surface and gently knead just until
it comes together, no more than 6 times. Pat dough into a 1-inch-thick
circle. Use a 1½-inch floured biscuit cutter to cut out biscuits—stamp
it into the dough; don't twist it—and arrange them about 1 inch apart on
prepared baking sheet.

For Assembly: Reserving the glaze in the skillet, press 1 sausage firmly
into the center of each biscuit. Bake until biscuits are golden, 12 to 15
minutes. Transfer baking sheet to a cooling rack. Bring glaze to a simmer
over medium heat, brush over biscuits, and serve warm.

Pairing Tip
For Pigs on Cushions, some of my
favorite drink pairings are Eve's
Addiction and the Shandy (pages 36
and 97).

Cheese-Crusted Olives

SERVES 4 TO 6

These single-bite appetizers are zesty, cheesy, and briny, a perfect punctuation to many of the sweet cocktails and punches in this book.

1 cup (4 ounces) crumbled feta cheese

4 tablespoons (½ stick) unsalted butter, softened

1 teaspoon finely grated lemon zest

1 ½ teaspoon za'atar*

½ teaspoon salt

¾ cup all-purpose flour

24 to 30 small pitted olives, such as Manzanillas

1 large egg yolk

1 tablespoon heavy cream

1 tablespoon black or white sesame seeds, or a combination

*This Middle Eastern condiment contains a number of seasonings, herbs, and spices such as sumac, sesame seeds, and za'atar itself, which is an herb similar to oregano. Look for it in specialty markets (see Sources, page 138).

Adjust an oven rack to the middle position and preheat oven to 375°F. Line a rimmed baking sheet with parchment paper.

In a large bowl, stir together cheese, butter, lemon zest, za'atar, and salt until thoroughly combined. Add flour and incorporate with hands until a dough is formed. Cover dough with plastic wrap and refrigerate for at least 15 minutes.

Scoop teaspoonfuls of dough and, using palms, roll into balls. With fingertips, flatten into 1½-inch circles. Place 1 olive on each disk, wrap dough around olive, and roll dough-covered olive between palms. Transfer to prepared baking sheet and refrigerate until firm, about 15 minutes. Whisk together egg yolk and cream. Brush mixture over dough-covered olives and sprinkle with sesame seeds.

Bake until golden, 20 to 25 minutes. Serve warm.

From time to time, I find stubborn olives with hard-to-remove pits. If you're in a similar situation, try serving them on a separate platter and provide a small bowl for discarded olive pits.

Roasted Marrow Bones

SERVES 6 TO 8

A restaurant staple, roasted marrow bones are easy to make at home. Use small spoons to scoop out the soft, intensely beefy marrow and serve it with fig compote or jam and crusty bread.

8 tablespoons kosher salt, divided

12 marrow bones, about 3 inches long, scraped clean*

Vegetable oil

Maldon salt, for serving

Fig compote or jam and crusty bread, for serving

Ask your butcher to trim the bones to size, or, for an alternative look, have him split the bones in half lengthwise. Scrape excess flesh from the outside of the bones for better presentation, using the dull side of a medium knife.

Twenty-four hours prior to roasting, combine 1 quart cold water and 2 tablespoons kosher salt in a large bowl. Add the bones and more water if needed to cover them by about 1 inch; refrigerate. Drain and rinse the bones about every 6 hours, replacing the saltwater solution each time. This will eliminate impurities and season the marrow.

Drain bones and pat dry. Adjust an oven rack to the middle position and preheat the oven to 450°F. Lightly oil a rimmed baking sheet and stand bones straight up on the prepared sheet. Roast for 20 to 30 minutes, or until the blade of a knife slips easily into the center cavity of each bone.

Transfer sheet to a cooling rack and let cool for about 5 minutes. Arrange the bones on a platter and sprinkle with Maldon salt. Serve them with compote or jam in a small bowl, along with crusty bread.

Give It a Try

To some, the idea of consuming the inside of a bone is sinister, but I am a firm believer in nose-to-tail eating. Once an animal has been sacrificed to the table, it is only proper to consume as much of it as possible. Bone marrow is soft, spreadable, and intensely beefy; it's no wonder that the dish is present on many haute dining menus. This recipe is easy to prepare and usually becomes the most talked about food at my parties. Serve with small spoons for easy scooping.

Acknowledgments

Where to begin? I grew up surrounded by women who welcomed me into their kitchens and always treated me like an adult. My grandmother Muriel Hüper de Argüello was, and remains, a willful beauty who reveled in entertaining and preparing elaborate meals. My paternal grandmother, Bertha Chamorro de Cuadra, is equally headstrong, inspiring, and full of humor. Both women come from what can best be described as a legacy of loss, but through it all, they remained the backbone of our families and nurtured through food and drink. I thank them for each lesson they have taught me. My grandfathers were equally responsible for instilling in me a love of food and drink. Dr. Silvio Cuadra Sáenz, the gentlest man alive, would take me to the market on Saturdays and then to his farm, where I learned to milk cows and not flinch at the sight of animals being slaughtered. He taught me fearlessness and compassion. Alejandro Argüello Sáenz, charmer, dancer, dandy, epicure . . . *Cuánta falta me hace.*

Thank you to my mother, María Argüello, who is everything to me: best friend, confidante, teacher. She instilled a passion for hard work and for all things beautiful and delicious. *Mami, te lo debo todo.*

Gracias a mi papá, José Cuadra Chamorro, y a mis hermanitos (los niños) José Alejandro, Juan Carlos y Eugenio, los hombres de mi vida quienes siempre me han apoyado y aguantado. Sin ustedes, sin su amor, sin su sentido de humor y pasión por la vida, no sería la misma.

Thank you to my husband, Octavio Sacasa Pasos, who deserves a medal for standing by me *en las duras y en las maduras.* You, sir, are my biggest fan and quietly watch and smile as I career through life, and for that you have all my love and gratitude. Thank you to my friends and family, who inspire me and bring tears to my eyes whenever they tell me they're proud of me: Judith Vanessa Pasos-Carreño, Meghan Erwin Hack, Meghan de Andrade, Alejandro Sacasa Pasos, Los Zampieri, Los Sacasa Pasos, Los Marín Pasos.

Thank you to everyone who was involved in the shoot and production of this book: my editor Margaret McGuire, designer Katie Hatz, the press team at Quirk Books, prop stylists Emily Rickard and Penelope Bouklas, unofficial PA Eric Martz, my better culinary half Dean Sheremet, Geraldine Pierson and Lea Siegel, and Good Light Studio.

Last, but not least, thank you Tara Striano. It feels like just yesterday that we were sitting on your balcony talking about the possibility of working on this book. Without your support, humor, and organization this wouldn't have happened. I love you, babe.

—*María del Mar*

First I'd like to thank my mother. You've been there for me at every turn, giving me the unerring support that only a mother can give. I wouldn't be writing this if it weren't for you, Mom. I love you. And Dad, if you were here I know you'd be so proud of me. Thank you to Eric Martz. Your love and support have been immeasurable. I couldn't have made it through this without you. You have been the best PA ever.

Thank you to Penelope Bouklas and Emily Rickard for creating the perfect canvases on which to make every shot beautiful. Your talents are limitless. Thank you to Geraldine Pierson for standing by my side, and for shooting our portrait for this book. We've been through a lot together, and I look forward to going through more. Thank you to Lea Siegel for making us look beautiful. Ferny Chung Studios, thank you so much. Your generosity helped make our portrait an amazing experience. We had a blast. A big thank you to the Bausches and to Benny and Pantera for offering your homes without blinking an eye. Thank you to Margaret McGuire, Katie Hatz, and everyone else at Quirk Books for making this book possible. Lastly, and most importantly, I want to thank María. I am so grateful for our connection. You are an amazing, creative individual; I am insanely lucky to have you in my life. Love you and everything you are.

—*Tara*

Sources

It doesn't take much to make a good winter cocktail. These shops are some of my favorite sources for cocktail ingredients, fridge and pantry basics, barware, and serveware.

Cocktail Kingdom
All things bar related: barware, serveware, ice trays, books, bitters, and syrups.
www.cocktailkingdom.com

Kalustyan's
Specialty international market carrying a wide array of dried goods and spices.
www.kalustyans.com

Mexgrocer
Specialty Latin American products.
www.mexgrocer.com

Penzeys Spices
Specialty spices.
www.penzeys.com

Sur La Table
Kitchen supplies, barware, serveware, and housewares.
www.surlatable.com

Tovolo
King-size and "perfect" square silicone ice cube trays, and other kitchen tools.
www.tovolo.com

Williams-Sonoma
Kitchen supplies, barware, serveware, and housewares.
www.williams-sonoma.com

Index

If you have enjoyed this book
or it has touched your life in some way,
we'd love to hear from you.

Please write a review at Hallmark.com,
e-mail us at booknotes@hallmark.com,
or send your comments to:
Hallmark Book Feedback
P.O. Box 419034
Mail Drop 100
Kansas City, MO 64141

Time for another round?

Hit up QuirkBooks.com/WinterCocktails to discover exclusive recipes we couldn't fit into the book, download printable recipe cards, find menus and checklists to help you plan your next cocktail party, read an exclusive Q&A with author María del Mar Sacasa and photographer Tara Striano, join the *Winter Cocktails* Pinterest board, and share your favorite seasonal drinks and snacks. Raise your glass and give a toast!